MUSTARD SEED SERIES

Christian Faith Formation
by
The Rev. A. E. Keire

**Curriculum Development
Associates, Inc.**

www.mustardseedseries.com

Cover Design: Tom Murphy
Illustrations: Barbara Wilkes

Curriculum Development Associates, Inc.
The Mustard Seed Series by
Rev. Anita E. Keire

ISBN: 9780998087726
2017 Edition

Biblical Time Line

Prehistory

Creation

Adam

Eve

Cain

Abel

Noah

Tower of Babel

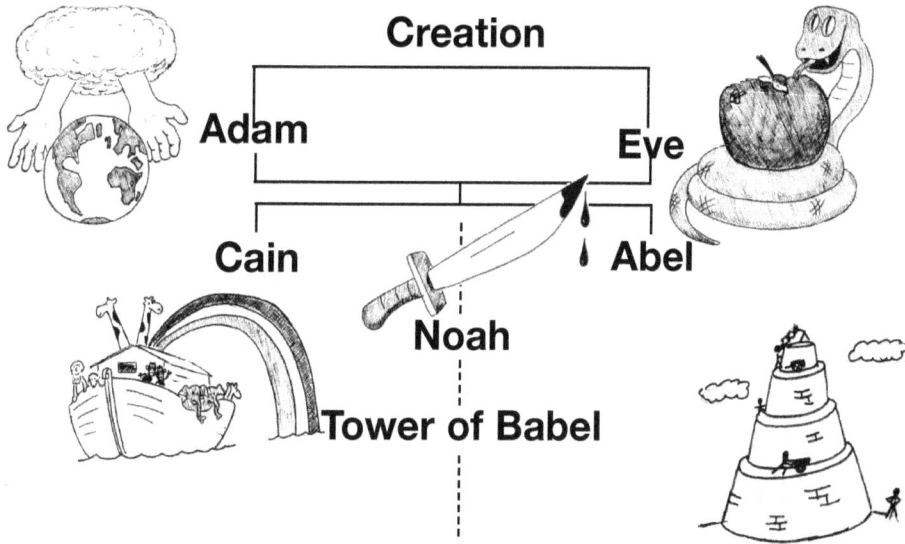

B.C. = everything that happened before Jesus was born

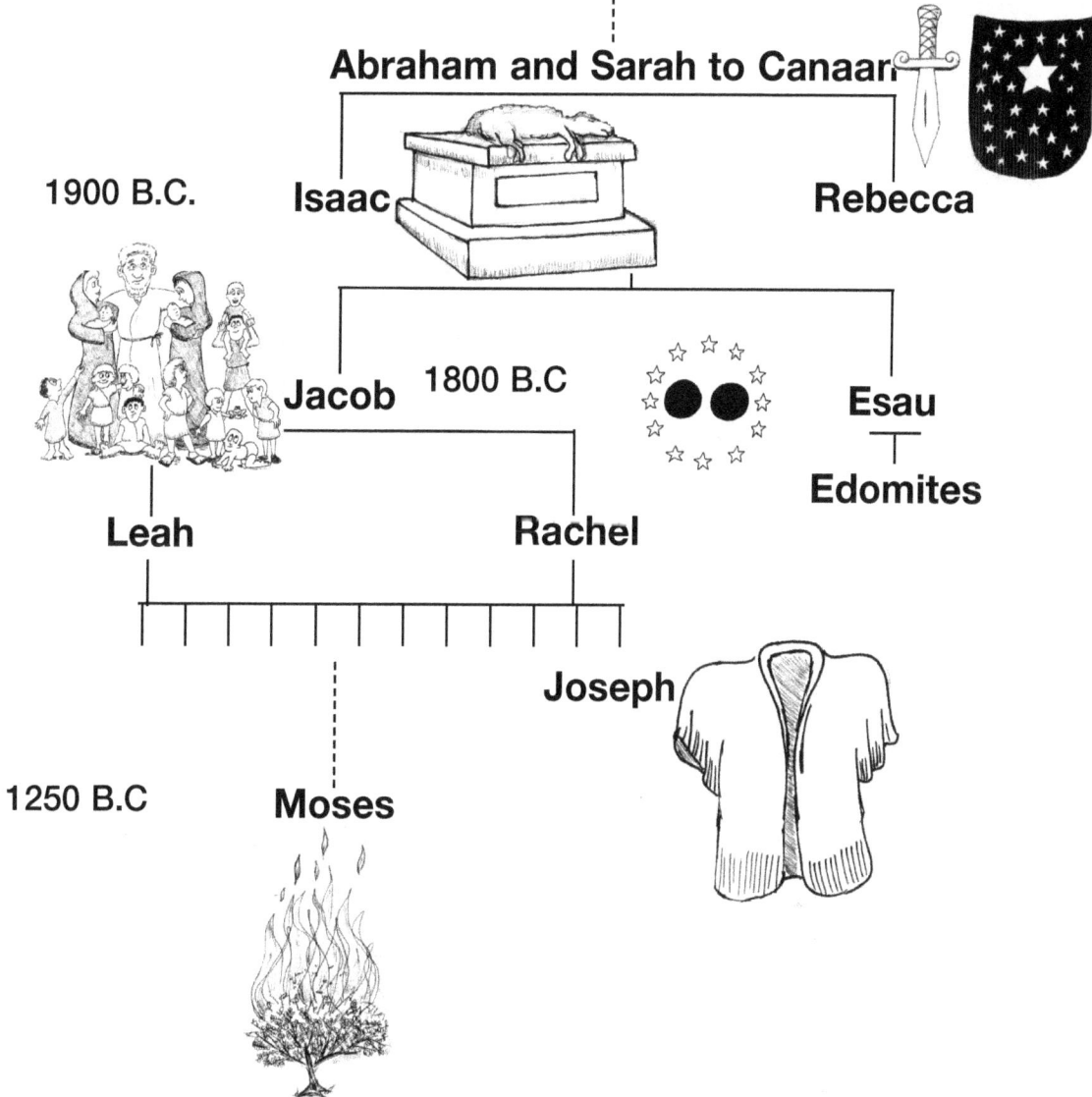

Abraham and Sarah to Canaan

1900 B.C.

Isaac

Rebecca

Jacob   1800 B.C

Esau

Edomites

Leah

Rachel

Joseph

1250 B.C

Moses

Biblical Time Line

From Moses to Jesus

1250 B.C.	**Moses** 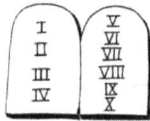	**Joshua** 	**Judges** 

1020 B.C.	**Saul**	**David** 	**Solomon** 

931 B.C.

Israelite kingdom divides.

Judah
Southern Kingdom

Israel
Northern Kingdom

865 B.C.

Rise of Prophets

722 B.C.   **Israel conquered by Assyrians.**

Biblical Time Line

586 B.C.   Judah conquered by Nebuchadrezzar of Babylonia. Exile in Babylonia.

538 B.C.   Cyrus of Persia conquers Babylonia. Allows exiles to return home.

334 B.C.   Alexander the Great's conquests begin. Greek rule begins.

164 B.C.   Judas Maccabeus defeats Greeks.

63 B.C.   Roman general Pompey conquers Israel.

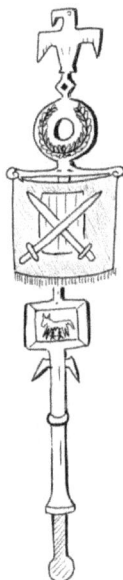

40 B.C.   Roman senate proclaims Herod, son of Antipater, King of Jews.

Biblical Time Line

7 B.C.   **Jesus is born.**

4 B.C.   **Herod dies.**

A.D. = *Anno domini* for the year of the Lord

28 A.D.   **John begins baptizing.**

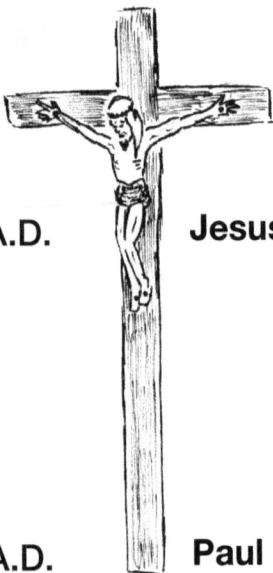

30 A.D.   **Jesus is crucified.**

33 A.D.   **Paul is converted.**

Seasons of the Church Year

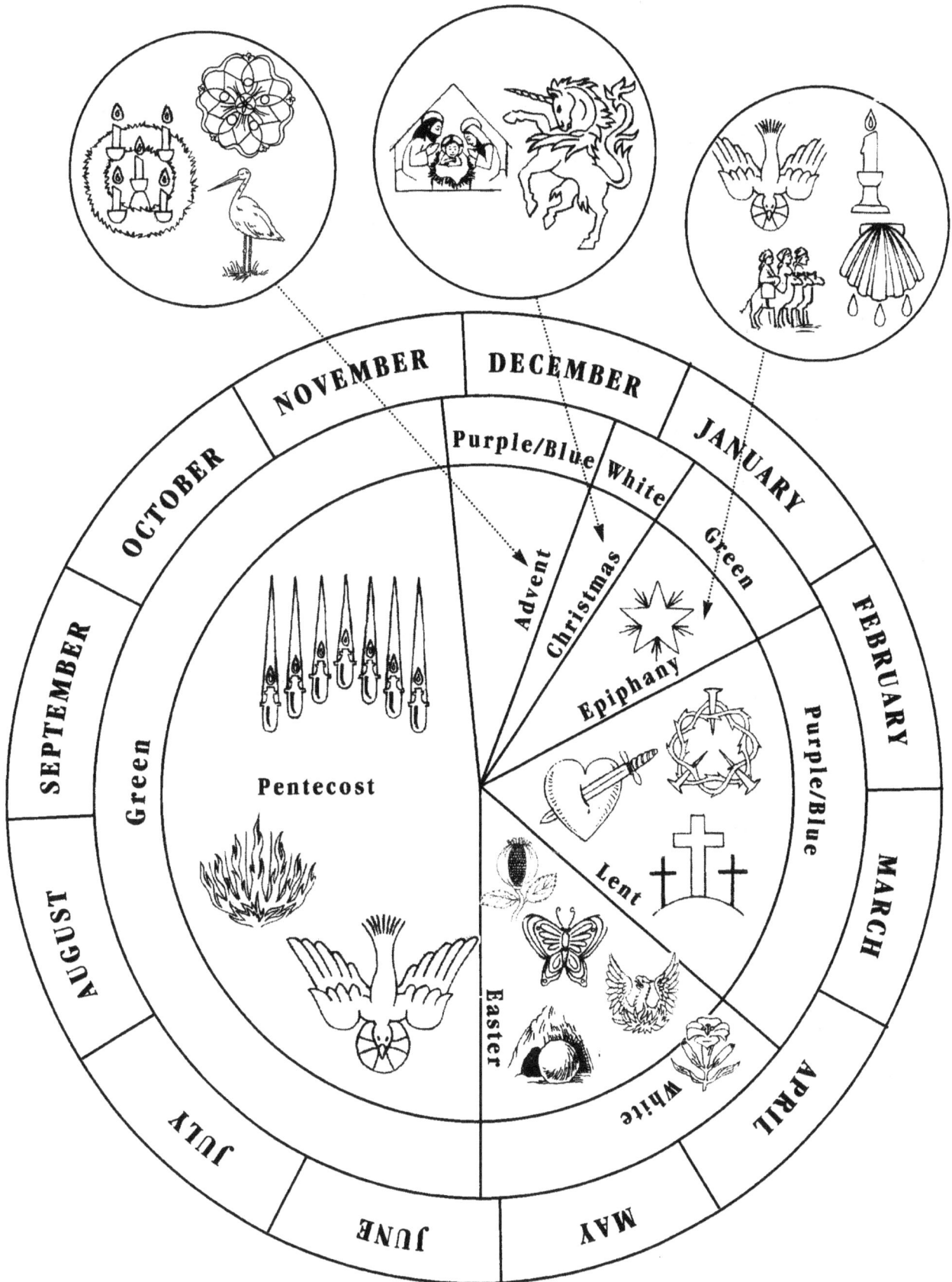

NOVEMBER
DECEMBER
OCTOBER
JANUARY
SEPTEMBER
FEBRUARY
AUGUST
MARCH
JULY
APRIL
JUNE
MAY

Purple/Blue
White
Green

Advent
Christmas
Epiphany

Green

Pentecost

Lent

Easter

Purple/Blue

White

Church Seasons

Advent is the first church season in the church calendar. We celebrate Advent during the four Sundays and weekdays before Christmas. During Advent we watch, wait, pray and prepare ourselves for the birth of Jesus.

The Advent Wreath is a symbol from northern Europe. It is an unadorned wreath made of evergreens, with four pink or purple candles in the outer rim and a white candle in the center of the wreath. The outer rim of candles represents the four Sundays before the birth of Jesus. The inner candle is the Christ candle, which is lighted on Christmas Eve or Christmas Day. It reminds us of Jesus' gifts of Peace, Hope, Love, and Joy.

The Rose represents the promise that God will send a Messiah.

The Stork represents watchfulness and is associated with Gabriel's invitation to Mary to become the mother of the Messiah.

The Colors for Advent are purple and/or blue. Purple symbolizes penitence, sorrow, or royalty. It also signifies love and truth. The color blue is Mary's color. Blue signifies purity, heaven, love, faithfulness, and truth.

Christmas follows Advent. Christmas is the shortest season in the church year, lasting only 12 days. It is a time for celebrating Jesus' birth and God's presence among us.

The Manger reminds us of the birth of Jesus.

The Unicorn represents purity, and is related to Mary and the birth of Jesus.

The Color for the Christmas season is white, which is a symbol for purity and joy.

Epiphany begins on January 6 with the visit of the Wise Men. The church season of Epiphany reminds us that Jesus came for all people and is a light in a dark world. It is a time for us to grow in our understanding and knowledge of Jesus.

The Five-Pointed Star represents the star the Wise Men followed to find Jesus. It also represents the fact that Jesus came not only to the Jewish people, but to everyone.

The Shell represents the baptism of Jesus by John the Baptist.

The Dove represents innocence and purity as well as the presence of the Holy Spirit at Jesus' baptism.

The Lighted Candle tells us that Jesus is the light of the world.

The Colors for Epiphany are white and green. White is used through the first Sunday following January 6. Thereafter green, which represents hope and new life, is used.

Church Seasons

Lent is a time for us to make a "U turn" in our lives if one is needed. Many of us need to seek inner spiritual cleansing which comes through our acknowledging disgust at our sins, our seeking forgiveness for them, and our living a new life in and through Jesus. Lent is a time to renew our commitment to our Lord Jesus Christ and to think about Jesus' great sacrifice.

Lent is 40 weekdays long. It begins on Ash Wednesday and ends on Good Friday. During Lent some Christians fast or eat very little food.

The Crown of Thorns represents the cruel crown that the soldiers pushed down on Jesus' head.

The Three Nails represent the nails that held Jesus to the cross.

The Heart Pierced by a Sword represents Mary's heart.

The Cross is what Jesus was crucified on.

The Colors for Lent are purple and/or blue. Red is used for Passion Sunday (Palm Sunday). White is used on Maundy Thursday. Black is for Good Friday.

Easter is the day we celebrate Jesus' resurrection from the dead. The Easter season lasts 50 days. Easter reminds Christians that they share in Jesus' victory over death. White is the color used for the Easter season. There are many symbols for Easter.

The Empty Cross tells us that Jesus is victorious over death.

The Phoenix became a symbol first for early Christians' belief in Jesus' resurrection and then for all Christians' resurrections. The phoenix was a large mythical bird that lived in the Arabian Desert. Legend has it that the phoenix was large like the eagle, and that it built its nests with twigs and spices and lived in it for 500 years. In the 500th year, the sun would set the nest afire. The phoenix would flap its wings to fan the fire, which eventually burned the phoenix to death. Shortly thereafter, the phoenix would rise from the dead, build a new nest and live another 500 years.

The Butterfly depicts new life. It goes through three different life stages. First, it is a caterpillar. Then it withdraws from the world into a chrysalis (cocoon) which it builds. From the cocoon it breaks out into a beautiful, mature butterfly. Jesus' life follows the butterfly's life stages. First, Jesus becomes a human and lives a simple existence. Then he dies and rests in the tomb. On the third day, Jesus rises gloriously from the dead with a new body.

The Open Tomb and Easter Lily represent Jesus' resurrection.

The Pomegranate with its many seeds in its fruit is symbolic of growth in the Word of God and the increase of God's grace.

White is the color for the Easter season and symbolizes purity and joy.

Church Seasons

Pentecost marks the beginning of the Christian Church. It is often called the birthday of the Church.

The Descending Dove represents peace and the Holy Spirit which came upon Jesus' disciples.

The Seven-Fold Flame represents peace and the Holy Spirit which came upon Jesus' disciples.

The Seven Lamps are the gifts of the Holy Spirit, which are

Wisdom
Understanding
Counsel
Spirit-Filled Strength
Knowledge
True Godliness
Holy Fear

The Fruits of the Spirit or Spirit in action are identified by Paul in his letter to the Galatians (5:22-23). They are love, joy, peace, patience, kindness, goodness, faithfulness, humility, and self-control.

Red is the color for Pentecost Sunday; it represents the color of fire. Red is also the color of blood spilled by the early Christian martyrs. Martyrs are people who were killed for their belief in Jesus.

Green is the color for the rest of the Pentecost season. Green is for growth in the Holy Spirit.

Biblical Time Line

Prehistory

Creation

Adam — Eve

Cain — Abel

Noah

Tower of Babel

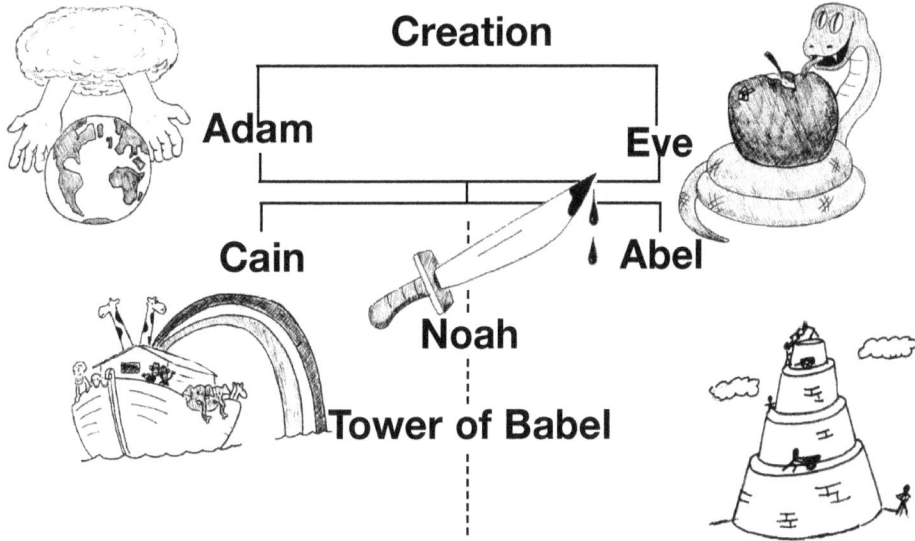

B.C. = everything that happened before Jesus was born

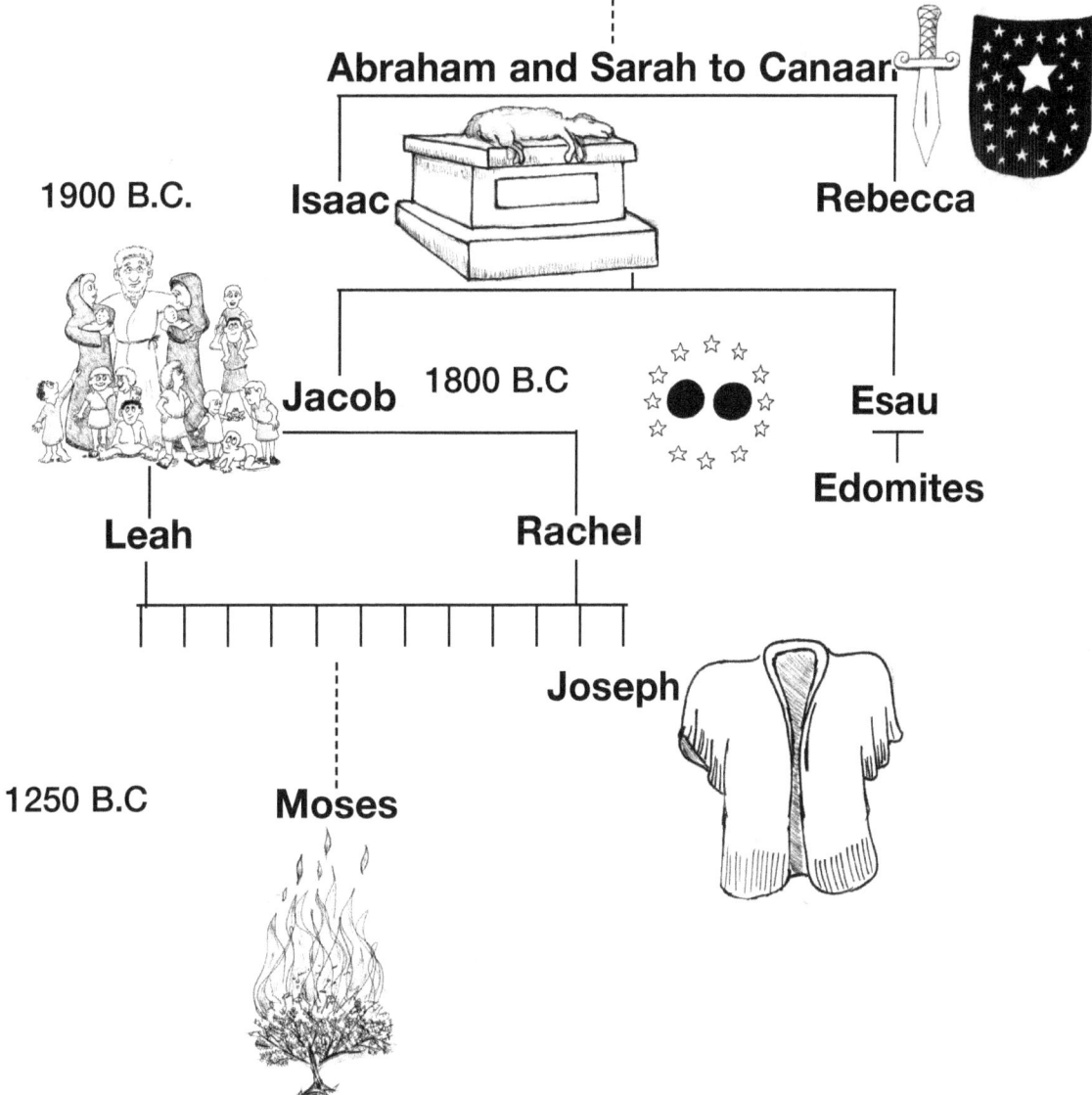

Abraham and Sarah to Canaan

1900 B.C.   Isaac — Rebecca

Jacob   1800 B.C   Esau — Edomites

Leah — Rachel

Joseph

1250 B.C   Moses

"Be strong and of good courage; be not frightened, neither be dismayed; for the Lord your God is with you wherever you go."

Joshua 1:9

GENESIS STORIES

```
D O E E G V H O A R A H P N
R U P N E I J M M G L Q P C
E P K I M P C A A S I U K M
A N U M I N S T E T Y I Y O
M H Q A P E A N O A H D B D
C C T F T J V N J K L E B A
O L Z A O F C I U P Z F M F
A S E S R V A A G E O M L P
T D E B X G I T R R N W R N
J P S F A D N A R K O X K N
H J H P V B T U Q E I F B G
U B O C A J V I G J D Q S A
U X G A G S L A V E R Y W L
F H V Y C R E A T I O N Z Y
```

ABEL	FORGIVE
ARK	ISAAC
BABEL	JACOB
CAIN	JOSEPH
CREATION	NOAH
DREAMCOAT	PHARAOH
FAMINE	SLAVERY

Nugget

Prayer is the belief that God exists, that there can be communication with God, and that God speaks to us through other people, events in life, nature, the prompting of the Holy Spirit, and through the Holy Bible.

A Note Home:

Today your child's class reviewed the book of Genesis. Next week we begin our study of Moses. It is important for your child to develop his/her spiritual life as well as an understanding of our faith story. The highlights of Chapters 1-3 in A Parent's Guide to Prayer were partially covered during our prayer time. Your help in guiding your child's spiritual life is needed. You may wish to purchase a copy of this book from Amazon.

How the Hebrews Came to Live and Be Enslaved in Egypt

Joseph, favored son of Jacob/Israel, was sold into slavery by ten of his brothers. For several years, Joseph served Potiphar, the captain of the palace guard, until he was falsely accused of a crime he did not commit and was thrown into prison.

While in prison, Joseph interpreted the dreams of Pharaoh's wine steward and chief baker. A few years later, he interpreted Pharaoh's dream of seven fat and sleek cows coming out of the Nile River only to be eaten by seven thin and bony cows. In another dream, Pharaoh saw seven heads of full and ripe grain be swallowed by seven heads of thin grain. All the wise men and magicians of the land could not interpret Pharaoh's dreams. Only Joseph could.

Pharaoh's dreams meant that there would be seven years of plenty followed by seven years of famine. Joseph suggested that one fifth of every crop during the years of plenty be collected, stored, and guarded. This surplus grain would provide food for Egypt during the famine.

In the second year of the famine, Joseph's brothers came to Egypt to buy food for their starving families. After testing them to find out whether they had become honest men, Joseph declared who he was and told his brothers and father to move to Egypt with their families.

Pharaoh gave them the fertile land of Goshen. Joseph's family benefited as did all Egyptians who lived near the Nile River with its yearly flooding and deposits of rich soil in which to raise their crops.

The total number of Jacob's male descendants who went into Egypt was 70. They increased greatly in number. By the time of Moses some 430 years later, there were 600,000 men, not counting women and children.

The Pharaohs of Egypt at the time of Joseph were not Egyptians but rather Hyksos (rulers of foreign uplands). They invaded Egypt from the East with horses and chariots. Before their arrival, Egypt had never seen horses. The Hyksos kings ruled for approximately 100 years from 1640 B.C. until they were driven out in 1585 B. C. by the local rulers of Thebes. Their greatest contribution to Egypt was the use of horse and chariot for aggressive military expansion and defense.

Land Walked by Our Faith Ancestors

The Egyptian population disliked the Hyksos. It is possible that the famine deepened this hostility towards the Hyksos Pharaohs and perhaps Joseph and his relatives. Joseph gave grain to the starving Egyptians in exchange for their freedom and land.

Events in the Book of Exodus are believed to have occurred during the 19th Dynasty (about 1350-1200 B.C.) during the reign of Seti I (1308-1290 B.C.) and Rameses II (1290-1224 B.C.)

Turn to and read Exodus 1. The word *exodus* means going out or departure. The Bible book Exodus tells us about the Hebrews' escape or going out from Egypt.

MEDITERRANEAN SEA

Cana Tiberias Lake Galilee
Nazareth
Samaria
mt. Gerizim
Arimathea
Jerusalem Bethany
Bethlehem
Dead Sea
NILE DELTA
Gaza
Rameses
Goshen
Pithom
Memphis
SINAI PENINSULA
Red Sea
Nile River
mt. sinai
Gulf of Aqaba
LAND OF MIDIAN

A Note Home:

Today your child reviewed events leading to the presence and then the enslavement of the Hebrews or Israelites in Egypt. S/he learned about the circumstances surrounding the birth of Moses, his escape to Midian and marriage to Zipporah, and the Egyptians' treatment of the Hebrews. Bible references were Exodus 1 and 2.

Moses and the Burning Bush

Domenico Fetti, *Moses and the Burning Bush*

"'Do not come any closer. Take off your sandals, because you are standing on holy ground. I am the God of your ancestors, the God of Abraham, Isaac, and Jacob.' So Moses covered his face, because he was afraid to look at God."

Exodus 3:5-6

- As an Egyptian prince, Moses probably knew little about God because he was raised by Egyptians who worshiped numerous gods. Jethro, Moses' father-in-law, was a priest and leader of the Midianite tribe called Kenites. It is through Jethro that Moses learned about God.

- Old Testament people believed that fire is the symbol for God's presence. The same applies to the pillar of cloud or smoke that guides the Hebrews out of Egypt. The burning bush also indicates the presence of God in that the bush is not consumed by the fire.

- Mideastern people, especially Moslems, remove their shoes before entering their houses of worship. This act is a sign of respect to God in the presence of God.

- At the burning bush, Moses is so awestruck by God's presence that he covers his head. Again, this action is a sign of respect. Until recently, women were required to wear hats in church. Even today, Jewish men cover their heads in their places of worship.

- At the burning bush, Moses seeks to find out God's name. By learning God's name, Moses thinks he may learn more about God and therefore have some power over God. God refuses to tell anything to Moses. God's response is "I AM WHO I AM." From this little revelation, the Israelites came to call God YHWH which was probably pronounced Yahweh which means "He causes to be." This name does not reveal anything about God's eternal being but only something about God's presence and activity in our lives.

- A hardened heart is a serious condition of unbelief, lack of faith, and even disobedience.

A Note Home:

   Today your child learned about Moses' call from God to lead God's people out of slavery and Moses' resistance to this call. The class finished their Bible covers which included a map for easy reference of Egypt, the Sinai Peninsula, and Israel. They also wrote their names in heiroglyphs for their Bible cover. Scripture references were Exodus 3-4:17 and prayer references were pages 67-74 in A Parent's Guide to Prayer.

Moses' Life

"I am the Lord; I will rescue you and set you free from your slavery to the Egyptians. I will raise my mighty arm to bring terrible punishment upon them, and I will save you. I will make you my own people, and I will be your God. You will know that I am the Lord your God when I set you free from slavery in Egypt."

Exodus 6:67

The Plagues

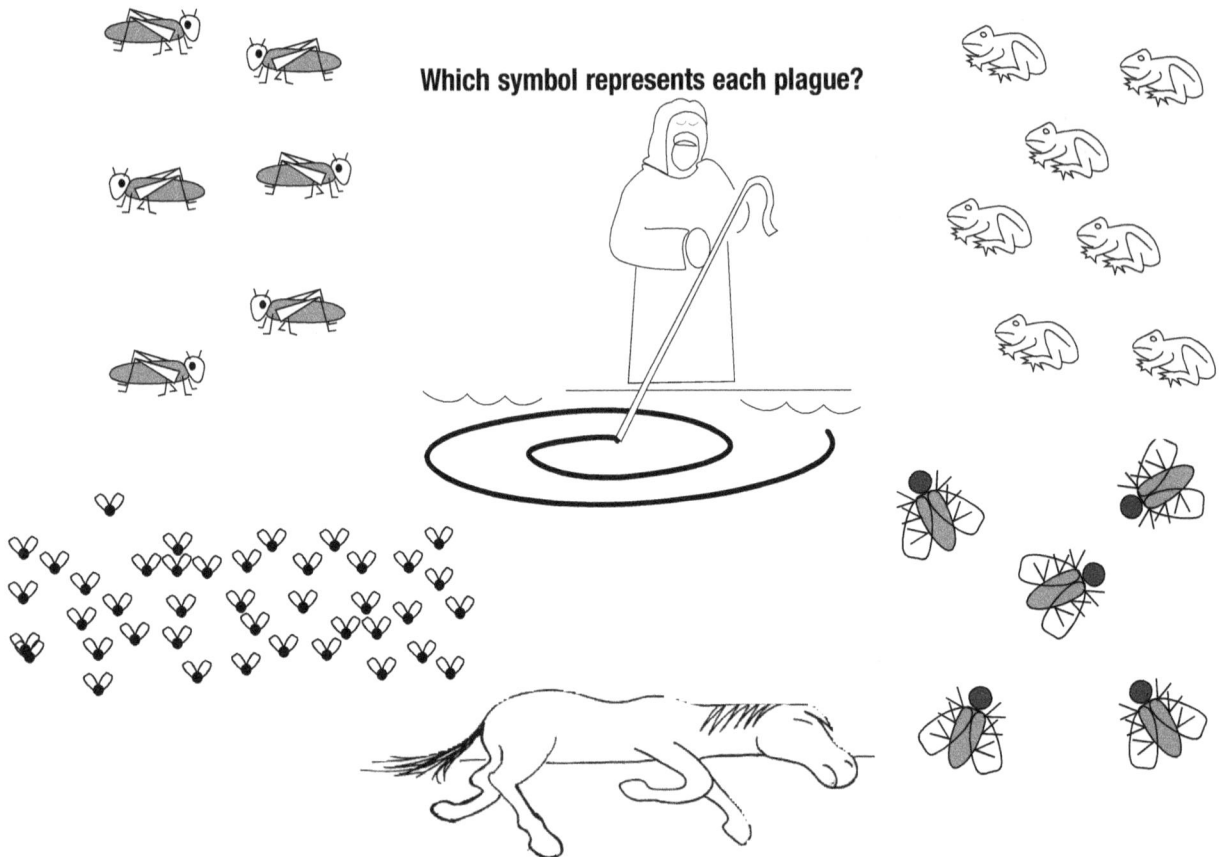

Which symbol represents each plague?

Nuggets

- Pharaoh believed he was the reincarnation of the Egyptian god Ra whom the Egyptians believed created the universe, humanity and other living things and creatures.

- Pharaoh thought Moses' God was powerless especially since Moses' God was the God of an enslaved people.

- The Egyptians believed in numerous gods and goddesses in addition to Pharaoh.

- Egyptians believed in an afterlife in which a dead person's soul needed his body and prized possessions in order to enjoy the afterlife.

- The plagues brought physical and psychological distress to the Egyptians.

- When a small "g" is used for god, this god is not the one, true God.

A Note Home:

Today your child learned of Moses' return to Egypt, of his reception and eventual rejection by the Hebrews because of Pharaoh's strike-breaking tactics, and transition from disbelief to belief of God's power on the part of the Hebrews and the Egyptians. Bible references were Exodus 4:18-9:7. Your child's class also started a diorama project on burial preparations for Pharaoh's first-born son.

Egyptians at the Time of Moses

The Hebrews living during the time of Moses were greatly influenced by Egyptian culture and Egyptian beliefs in numerous gods. Hebrew understanding and knowledge of the God of Abraham, Isaac, and Jacob were shallow at best. No doubt the Hebrews were drawn to and flirted with the Egyptian gods.

Our God had to prove to the Hebrews that the Egyptian gods were no match to our God. God wanted to remove the Hebrews from this idolatrous society and reshape them away from Egyptian society so that they could truly become God's people.

The Egyptians believed in numerous gods and goddesses. These gods often took on the characteristics of birds and animals. Each god served a particular purpose in ordering the world and influencing the lives of the people.

Ra

Hathor

The Egyptians' main god was Ra, the sun god, upon whom all life depended. Ra was sometimes called Amen-Ra. Egyptians believed he was the creator of the world, of people, and everything else within the world. Ra took on the shape of a man and became Egypt's first Pharaoh. He caused the Nile to rise and flood the land and to leave rich deposits of soil for producing fine crops. Ra lived for over a thousand years. He was the first Pharaoh and was believed to be reincarnated in succeeding Pharaohs. In other words, Pharaoh was god. Pharaoh was the absolute ruler and no one dared question his authority.

Ma'at

Egyptians believed that a dead person's soul needed his body and his most prized possessions of his worldly life to go with him into his tomb in order to be able to survive and enjoy life in the afterlife and the world of the dead. Wall paintings and hieroglyphs were thought to possess magical powers and covered the walls of tombs. Everything placed in a tomb helped preserve the body spirit and the winged soul. The winged soul was free to roam the Underworld and could return to earth so long as his body spirit survived.

Anubis

Nefertem

Egyptians believed that an underworld existed called Duat. They believed that life could continue indefinitely there provided certain precautions were taken during life. Rich Egyptians and Pharaohs were the only ones financially able to take these precautions for the afterlife. They had to build tombs that were secured against grave robbers. Within these tombs, the mummified corpse was placed inside double or triple coffins that portrayed the individual as he would like to look for eternity.

The underworld or next life or the Kingdom of the West was believed to be a happy land somewhere in the West. Entry into this land required the dead person to be properly mummified with his heart and various organs encased in Canopic jars. The dead person had to convince the ferryman to carry him across the River of Death. Then the dead person had to go through twelve gates guarded by serpents and through the Lake of Fire. An instruction book called the *Book of the Dead* told him how to bypass these dangers and what spells and incantations had to be used.

Egyptians at the Time of Moses

When the dead person arrived at the Judgment Hall of Azores, he was brought forward by Anubis, the jackal-headed god of mummification (on the left-hand side of the picture on the previous page). On the top of the picture there are 42 assessors who accuse the dead person of crimes he committed in his lifetime. He would have to deny these crimes. To determine whether a dead person's heart were pure and whether he had done good deeds in his lifetime, the dead person's heart would then be weighed in the Hall of Two Truths. His heart would be on one side of the scale and the feather of truth on the other side of the scale. Then the god of wisdom, Toth, declared in his book whether the dead person were innocent or not. If found guilty, the dog-like figure known as the Devourer of the Dead would eat the dead person's heart. Without his heart, the dead person would not survive the afterlife. If found innocent, the dead person would go before Azores, the god of the Underworld, who would permit this person to enter his kingdom where he would live in the Fields of the Blessed.

King Tutankhamun and his wife Ankesenpaaton.

In 1922, Howard Carter, a British archaeologist, discovered King Tutankhamun's tomb. King Tutankhamun reigned from 1334-1325 B.C. He had three golden coffins inside an outer, large stone sarcophagus (name for a stone coffin). The first two outer coffins were made of carved wood covered with gold leaf. The inner most coffin was made out of solid gold and weighed over 220 pounds. Each coffin presented an idealized portrait of the dead Pharaoh with certain representations of gods or goddesses and hieroglyphs protecting the dead person's body.

Goddesses at each end of the sarcophagus protect King Tutankhamun.

Make a fairly large diorama to be completed three Sundays from today. You may wish to go to your local library to get more information on Ancient Egypt's burial practices.

The last plague that God pronounced on the stubborn Egyptians was the death of the firstborn son. Pharaoh's son died on the night the Angel of Death passed over the Hebrews' homes.

Pretend that you are Egyptians working for Pharaoh. You are directed by Pharaoh to oversee the preparation of his son's body, his son's tomb, and his possessions to be placed in the tomb. Decide among yourselves who will do what. For instance,

- What will Pharaoh's son's coffin look like?
- What will be written and drawn on the coffin?
- What will be written and drawn on the walls?
- What spells and incantations will be needed in the *Book of the Dead* for safe passage into the underworld?
- What will the inner entrance gate have on it?
- Should his tomb be carved out of the side of the hill?
- How will you secure the tomb from grave robbers?
- Write a simple script or play to be read at the time of burial assuring Pharaoh that all precautions for the survival of his son in the afterlife have been taken.

You will probably need cardboard boxes, plenty of clay for people and coffins, white paper for drawing pictures and hieroglyphs for the walls of the tomb, for covering the coffins, the *Book of the Dead* (be sure to roll it as a scroll). All wall writing was done in different colors so you will need paint, too.

Good luck!

Inside a burial chamber of the 19th dynasty

Whose God Is in Charge?

"The Lord then said to Moses, 'Raise your hand toward the sky, and a darkness thick enough to be felt will cover the land of Egypt.'"

Exodus 10:21

CHEOP'S PYRAMID

Instructions: Find the burial chamber

Nuggets

- **Moses was unsure of himself and not a good speaker**
- **He did not want to assume the tasks God placed on him for fear of failure.**
- **Only after Moses developed faith and trust in God did he become a confident and determined leader.**

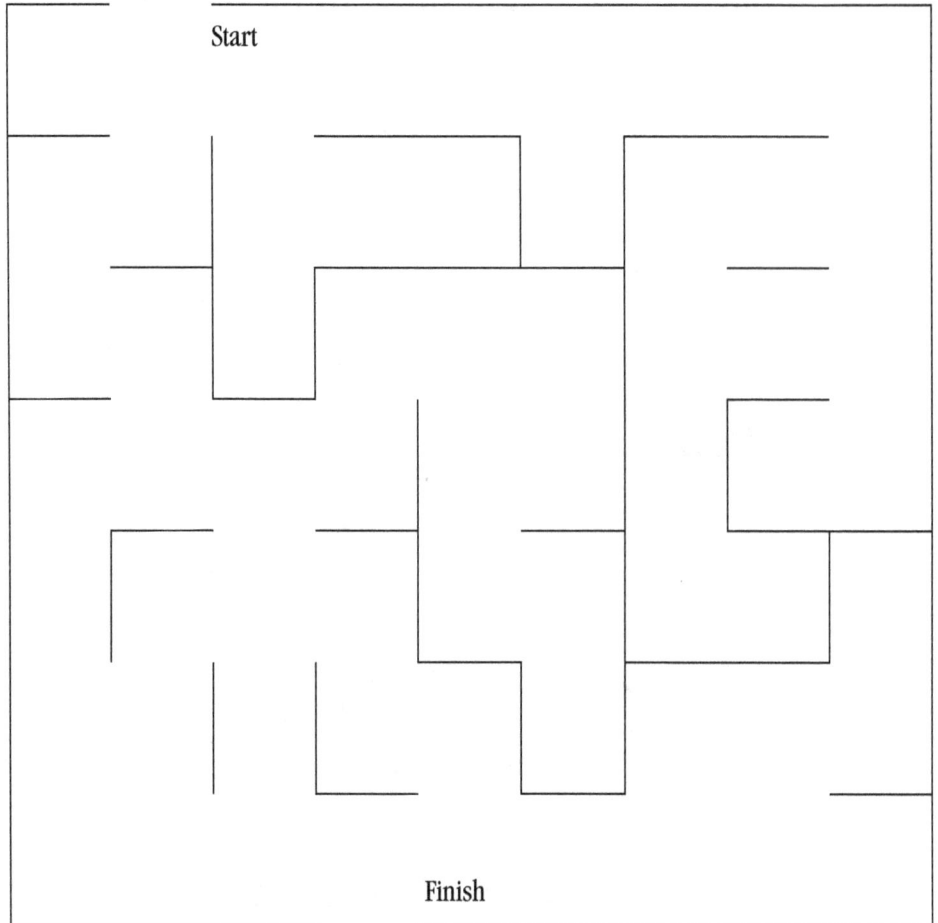

Start

Finish

A Note Home:

    Today your child learned about four more plagues that afflicted the Egyptian people and their recognition that the Hebrews' God was more powerful than Pharaoh. The class continued to work on their diorama project. Biblical references were Exodus 9:8-10:29.

Moses Crossing the Red Sea

15th Century Woodcut from the Gutenberg Bible

"When the Israelites saw the great power with which the Lord had defeated the Egyptians, they stood in awe of the Lord; and they had faith in the Lord and in his servant Moses."

Exodus 14:31

THE GREAT EXODUS

CLOUD　　　　　GOD

DISBELIEF　　　JEWELRY

DOORPOSTS　　MOSES

EXODUS　　　　PASSOVER

FAITH　　　　　PHARAOH

FEAR　　　　　PLAGUE

FIRE　　　　　SEA OF REEDS

FIRSTBORN　　STUBBORN

```
A Y D M F E X O D U S W S K
N C A I E D S L Z E D E S B
I R H Y A Z O T A Q S P Q V
O N O O R G J O U O F I I E
D S X B A L F E M B E E P W
I O R R T R E M U I B R I Y
S H X E E S A W C G W O I U
B H U E V F R H E Y A F R F
E V D M A O W I P J P L X N
L S Q I C U S R F Y T H P O
I B T V L S T S O P R O O D
E H R I O I X P A R D P J M
F Y J Q U U L X W P T O P C
X P F L D I X U R S A R G G
```

Nuggets

- Pharaoh did not want to recognize the Hebrews' God because it would have been an admission that he was a powerless god next to God.

- The Passover is one of the Jewish people's holiest holidays. It is a celebration of their deliverance from Egyptian bondage through God's divine intervention.

- Symbolically, the pillar of cloud and the pillar of fire signify the presence of God.

- To help us know God better, religious holidays are supposed to help us relive a past event such as the Passover and the exodus or escape from Egypt.

- Moses gives good advice to the frightened and pursued Hebrews that can be helpful to us today. Moses says in Exodus 14:13, "Don't be afraid! Stand your ground, and you will see what the Lord will do to save you today."

A Note Home:

Today your child learned of the origins of Passover, the tenth plague inflicted by God on the Egyptians, the Hebrews' exodus from Egypt. They spent the rest of the day preparing for next week's presentation of the burial of Pharaoh Ramesses II's son. Scripture references were Exodus 11-14.

The Wardrobe

Nuggets

C.S. Lewis' book *The Lion, the Witch and the Wardrobe* is considered by some people to be a fairy tale because magic, disguises, and spells are a part of the story.

- It is taught in the public schools as a fairy tale although in fact C.S. Lewis intended it to be a Christian allegory.

- An *allegory* is "a story in which people, things, and happenings have a hidden or symbolic meaning. Allegories are used for teaching or explaining ideas and moral principles" *(New World Dictionary)*.

The following objects are symbols in the story. What could they represent? How would you represent them?

- Narnia

- Snow

- The Wardrobe

- Mr. Tumnus' cave

- The lamppost

- Music

Narnia

Christian Skredsvig, 1914, *Winter Night in Rondane*

"I am the light of the world…Whoever follows me will have the light of life and will never walk in darkness."

John 8:12

A Note Home:

   Today your child began our study of C.S. Lewis' The Lion, the Witch and the Wardrobe *as a Christian allegory. For next week, they are to read chapters 3-6.*

Mr Tumnus' Cave Before Fenris Ulf

"The greatest love a person can have for his friends is to give his life for them."

John 15:13

The White Witch of Narnia

The following people and things represent hidden meanings or symbols in the story. What could they possibly represent? How would you represent them?

- The White Witch

- Turkish Delight

- Edmund

- Lucy, Susan, and Peter

- Winter without any Christmas

- The professor

- The robin

"Something beautiful and attractive has the possibility of being evil as well."

A. E. Keire

A Note Home:

Today your child continued an in-depth analysis of the Christian allegory The Lion, the Witch and the Wardrobe. *Self interest, truth, falsehood, friendship, and their consequences were discussed. Next week's reading assignment is Chapters 7-11.*

Edmund's Journey

Trust in the Lord

"Trust in the Lord with all your heart. Never rely on what you think you know. Remember the Lord in everything you do, and he will show you the right way. Never let yourself think that you are wiser than you are; simply obey the Lord and refuse to do wrong."

Proverbs 3:5-7

The following people, creatures or things represent some hidden meaning or symbol in *The Lion, the Witch and the Wardrobe*. What could they possibly represent?

- Edmund's betrayal

- Father Christmas

- The grey wolf Fenris Ulf

- Stone statues

A Note Home:

Today your child continued learning more about events and creatures in Narnia and how they closely resemble events and people in our world. Trust, mistrust and betrayal were discussed. Please encourage your child to read chapters 12-14 for next week.

The Death of Aslan

"People passing by shook their heads and hurled insults at Jesus: 'Aha! You were going to tear down the Temple and build it back up in three days! Now come down from the cross and save yourself!'"

Mark 15:29-30

Edmund's Close Call

Nuggets

- *Sin* is a separation from God which most often reflects itself in wrong attitudes and deeds.

- *Sin* is doing what we know we ought not to do and not doing what we ought to do.

- *Forgiveness* is the ability to not hold someone accountable for his misdeeds or bad things he does towards another person.

- *Repentance* is sorrow for the wrongdoing we committed. It is an admission of fault and a resolve to live a better life. Repentance is also an attempt to right wrongs committed. True repentance brings us into a new and better relationship with God.

- Jesus *redeems* us and sets us free from our sins.

A Note Home:

  Today your child discussed the struggle between good and evil, sin, repentance, forgiveness, and redemption as they applied to Aslan in The Lion, the Witch and the Wardrobe *and to Jesus' life. We also made Thanksgiving Prayer Links and joined them together into one long prayer.*

God is Known to Us
Through the Trinity

Nuggets

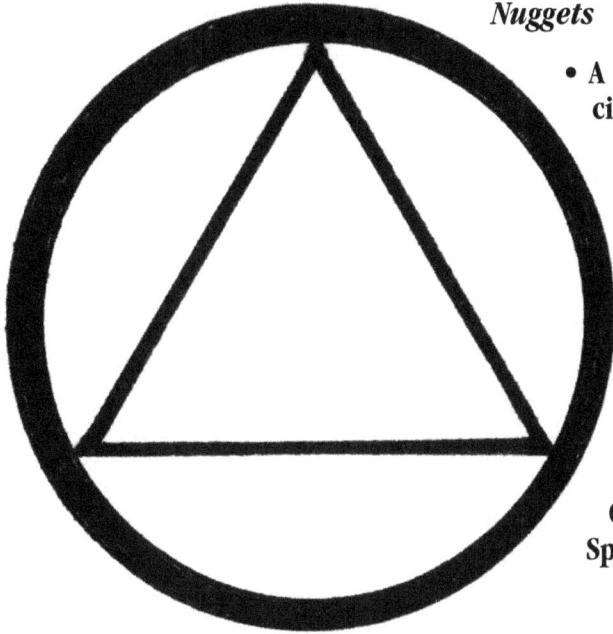

- A circle has no beginning and no end. A true circle lasts forever.

- We represent God by a triangle inside a circle.

- The triangle is symbolic of the three distinct roles of God known to us as the Father, Son, and Holy Spirit. The triangle is the symbol used for the Trinity.

- We also refer to the Trinity as God the Creator of the universe, God the Redeemer of humankind found in the Son known as Jesus Christ, and God the Sustainer known as the Holy Spirit or God's presence with us.

Waiting for Jesus

O COME, O COME, EMMANUEL

O come, O come, Emmanuel,
And ransom captive Israel,
That mourns in lonely exile here
Until the Son of God appear.

Refrain:
Rejoice! Rejoice!
Emmanuel shall come to thee, O Israel.

O come, O come, thou Rod of Jesse, free
Thine own from Satan's tyranny;
From depths of hell thy people save,
And give them victory o'er the grave.

Refrain

O come, thou Dayspring, come and cheer
Our spirits by thine advent here;
Disperse the gloomy clouds of night,
And death's dark shadows put to flight.

Refrain

O come, thou Key of David, come,
And open wide our heav'nly home;
Make safe the way that leads on high,
And close the path to misery.

Refrain

Nuggets

- **Each year we talk about the importance of the birth of Jesus.**
- **Jesus comes to bring us the good news from God.**
- **Each year Jesus calls us to let him into our lives.**
- **Advent is a special time of waiting, watching, praying, and preparing ourselves for entering Jesus' world as he encountered it and came to know and understand it.**
- **Advent is a time to let Jesus enter our world.**

A Note Home:

    Today your child concluded his/her study of the Christian allegory of The Lion, the Witch and the Wardrobe. *We talked about the similarities between Jesus and Aslan and the concept of the Incarnation and the Trinity. You may wish to read Chapter 9 in* A Parent's Guide to Prayer *for more information.*

The Messiah Shall Free Us

The people who walked in darkness have seen a great light.
They lived in a land of shadows, but now light is shining on them.
You have given them great joy, Lord; you have made them happy.
They rejoice in what you have done,…. For you have broken the
yoke that burdened them and the rod that beat their shoulders. A
child is born to us! A son is given to us! And he will be our ruler.
He will be called, 'Wonderful Counselor,' 'Mighty God,' 'Eternal
Father,' 'Prince of Peace.' His royal power will continue to grow; his
kingdom will always be at peace. He will rule as King David's suc-
cessor, basing his power on right and justice, from now until the
end of time. The Lord Almighty is determined to do all this."

Isaiah 9:2-7

O COME, O COME, EMMANUEL

O come, O come, Emmanuel,
And ransom captive Israel,
That mourns in lonely exile here
Until the Son of God appear.

Refrain:
Rejoice! Rejoice!
Emmanuel shall come to thee, O Israel.

O come, O come, thou Rod of Jesse, free
Thine own from Satan's tyranny;
From depths of hell thy people save,
And give them victory o'er the grave.

Refrain

O come, thou Dayspring, come and cheer
Our spirits by thine advent here;
Disperse the gloomy clouds of night,
And death's dark shadows put to flight.

Refrain

O come, thou Key of David, come,
And open wide our heav'nly home;
Make safe the way that leads on high,
And close the path to misery.

Refrain

Nuggets

The Jewish people believed the Messiah would destroy their enemies and establish a glorious earthly kingdom. They did not expect their Messiah to be a man of peace and born to a peasant woman.

God speaks to us through the Bible and through other people. All we have to do is look for God's messages to us. Look for God's clues and hints. We will find God if we look.

A Note Home:

Today your child learned of Isaiah's prophecy of the Messiah (Isaiah 9:2-7), of Jesus' announcement why he came into the world (Luke 4:16-30), of his rejection by the people of Nazareth, of the contradictions in people's expectations then and now. They heard a parallel story of a despairing shoemaker.

Encountering and Receiving Jesus in Our Hearts

"The Spirit of the Lord is upon me, because he has chosen me to bring good news to the poor.

He has sent me to proclaim liberty to the captives and recovery of sight to the blind, to set free the oppressed and announce that the time has come when the Lord will save his people."

Luke 4:18-19

GOD'S REVELATION

```
W O D A H S H O A R A H P N
R U P N K I N G D O M Q P C
E P K D E S S E R P P O K M
S N U M I N S T E R Y I Y O
D H J A P L I B E R T Y B D
R S U S E J V R J K L E B A
E L S A I F I I U P Z C H F
H S T S R G R E G N A M P P
P D I B H G H T R P C P E N
E P C T A D N T T A E X S N
H J E P V B H I Q A I F O G
S I G H T G V I C J D Q J A
U X G A I E L E M A R Y W L
F H V L C R E A T I O N Z Y
```

CAPTIVE   SHADOW

LIBERTY   PEACE

SIGHT   KINGDOM

JESUS   RIGHT

MANGER   JUSTICE

SHEPHERDS   MARY

OPPRESSED   JOSEPH

LIGHT

O COME, O COME, EMMANUEL

O come, O come, Emmanuel,
And ransom captive Israel,
That mourns in lonely exile here
Until the Son of God appear.

Refrain:
Rejoice! Rejoice!
Emmanuel shall come to thee, O Israel.

O come, O come, thou Rod of Jesse, free
Thine own from Satan's tyranny;
From depths of hell thy people save,
And give them victory o'er the grave.

Refrain

O come, thou Dayspring, come and cheer
Our spirits by thine advent here;
Disperse the gloomy clouds of night,
And death's dark shadows put to flight.

Refrain

O come, thou Key of David, come,
And open wide our heav'nly home;
Make safe the way that leads on high,
And close the path to misery.

Refrain

A Note Home:

    Today your child learned about the birth of Jesus in a stable, about the announcement of Jesus' birth to the shepherds and their arrival in the stable; they heard the conclusion to "The Shoemaker Michael," which offered clues on how Jesus comes to us today. Scripture references were Luke 2:1-20 and 4:18-19.

Adoration of the Wise Men

Adoration of the Wise Men, Albrecht Dürer

"Bethlehem in the land of Judah, you are by no means the least of the leading cities of Judah; for from you will come a leader who will guide my people Israel."

Matthew 2:6

The Flight into Egypt

"Herod will be looking for the child in order to kill him. So get up, take the child and his mother and escape to Egypt, and stay there until I tell you to leave."

Matthew 2:13

Carpaccio, 1500, *The Flight into Egypt*

A Note Home

Today your child reviewed the historical events leading up to the birth of Jesus, learned about the Wise Men's visit, of Herod's slaughter of the children, of Mary's, Joseph's, and Jesus' flight to Egypt (Matthew 2). S/he also reviewed the first three church seasons in the liturgical calendar.

John Baptizes Jesus

"While Jesus was praying, heaven was opened, and the Holy Spirit came down upon him in bodily form like a dove. And a voice came from heaven, 'You are my own dear Son. I am pleased with you.'"

Luke 3:21-22

The Doxology

OLD HUNDREDTH (Altered Rhythm) L. M.

Praise God from whom all bless-ings flow; Praise Him, all crea-tures here be-low;

Praise Him a-bove, ye heaven-ly host: Praise Fa-ther, Son, and Ho-ly Ghost. A-MEN.

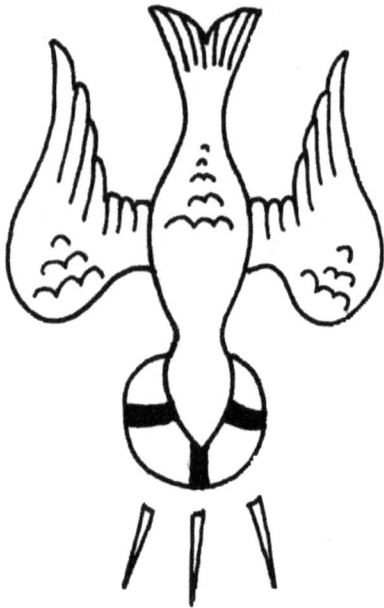

Nuggets

- The desert or the wilderness reminds people of the Israelites' wanderings before they entered the Promised Land. During that time, God was forming them into a nation and a faith community. The wilderness is a place where people can go to find their spiritual roots.

- John the Baptist's message is
  - Turn away from your sins,
  - Be baptized as a sign of your desire to live a new life,
  - Then God will forgive you of your sins.

- John tells us: "Whoever has two shirts must give one to the man who has none, and whoever has food must share it" (Luke 3:11).

A Note Home:

Today your child learned about the strange events surrounding the conception and birth of John the Baptist, of his relationship to Jesus, about repentance and sharing. They also heard a story about sharing called "The Bus Stop." Scripture references were Luke 1 and 3:1-22.

The Temptation of Christ

Duccio di Buoninsegna, *The Temptation of Christ*

"Jesus returned from the Jordan full of the Holy Spirit and was led into the desert, where he was tempted by the Devil for forty days."

Luke 4:1-2

A Note Home:

   Today your child studied the three temptations of Jesus in the Wilderness and drew parallels to similar modern-day temptations. Jesus went into the wilderness to pray and seek God's help in deciding the shape, purpose, and direction for his ministry. The scriptural text was Luke 4:1-13.

THE THREE TEMPTATIONS OF JESUS—THREE POWER ISSUES

1. "If you are God's son, order this stone to turn into bread" (Luke 4:3).
   - This temptation challenges the social and interior needs of people.
   - It holds up materialism against the Word of God.
   - It contrasts physical hunger to spiritual hunger.
   - Jesus' answer was people cannot live on bread alone.

2. "I will give you all this power and all this wealth … All this will be yours, then, if you worship me" (Luke 4:6-7).
   - Dictatorship or world dominance was unacceptable to Jesus.
   - Earthly power and possessions form a wall between God and people.
   - Jesus' response was that we are to worship the Lord our God and serve only God.

3. "If you are God's Son, throw yourself down from here…'God will order his angels to take good care of you'" (Luke 4:9-10).
   - Spectacles do not create an enduring faith.
   - Jesus wanted people to respond to his message and to who he was and nothing else.
   - Jesus told the Devil not to put the Lord your God to the test.

Jesus' Early Ministry

- We know that Jesus was baptized by John.

- He fasted for 40 days in the wilderness and was tempted by the Devil.

- After these temptations, Jesus goes into Galilee and teaches in the synagogues.

- He goes to the synagogue in Nazareth, his hometown, and proclaims the purpose of his mission which is to

  - Bring good news to the poor,
  - Proclaim liberty to the captives,
  - Restore sight to the blind,
  - Set free the oppressed,
  - Proclaim the time has come for the Lord to save his people.

- Jesus is almost killed by the hometown folks.

- He continues to preach and teach in the synagogues throughout Galilee.

- He heals the sick.

- He speaks with authority and becomes popular among the common people.

- The number of his followers increases.

- Many people call Jesus *rabbi* which means *teacher.* Jesus, like all teachers of his time, gathers students about him with the understanding that they in turn would someday teach others.

- Jesus calls disciples who have different backgrounds, skills, personalities, and talents.
  The first disciples he calls are fishermen.

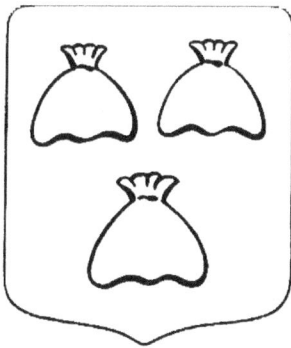

WHAT QUALIFICATIONS WOULD A TAX COLLECTOR HAVE AS A FUTURE CHURCH LEADER?

WHAT QUALIFICATIONS WOULD FISHERMEN HAVE AS FUTURE CHURCH LEADERS?

Apostles are the 12 men selected from Jesus' disciples to form his inner circle. The apostles will be the leaders of the early Church.

Seuola di San Giorgio degli Schiavoni, 1502, *The Calling of St. Matthew*

A Note Home:

   Today your child learned about Jesus' call to his first disciples, their accepting the call (Luke 5:1-11, 27-31), and the meaning of Our Father, who art in heaven *in the Lord's Prayer. You may want to read more on the Lord's Prayer by reading Chapter 6 of* A Parent's Guide to Prayer.

Christ Healing a Leper

Rembrandt, *Christ Healing a Leper*

"Sir, if you want to, you can make me clean!"

Luke 5:12

Nugget

Miracles are difficult for people to understand for the following reasons.

- **Miracles contradict natural law or the known laws of nature.**
- **Christians believe that the miracles Jesus performed were caused by God through Jesus.**
- **Most of Jesus' miracles required belief or faith on the part of the one to be healed.**
- **Miracles tell us something about God.**
- **Miracles send us a message from God. It is for us to determine what that message is.**

A Note Home:

Today your child learned about Jesus' healing of a leper (Luke 5:12-16), about miracles, about interior defilement (Mark 7:14-23), ceremonial purification, and the meaning of Hallowed be thy name *in the Lord's Prayer. You may want to continue studying Chapter 6 in* A Parent's Guide to Prayer.

Evil Thoughts Make a Person Unclean

- The word *hallowed* means *holy*. Something that is holy is set apart and regarded with awe. To hallow God's name means to regard God's name and God with awe and as the most sacred, holy, valuable name in all the universe.

- When people mix God's name or Jesus' name with foul curses and oaths, the prophets say that God weeps. People who curse hold God and God's will in low regard. The prophets and Jesus say there will be a Judgment Day when we all have to account for our behavior.

"It is what comes out of a person that makes him unclean."

Mark 7:20

Taken from a twelfth-century Winchester Bible.

The Legend of St. Valentine

Many, many years ago and long after Jesus was crucified by Roman soldiers, Roman Emperor Claudius II ordered all people to worship 12 Roman gods. Christians refused to worship false gods such as the Roman gods. They were faithful followers of Jesus and worshipped only God.

A Christian by the name of Valentinus was arrested, imprisoned, and sentenced to death because he would not worship the Roman gods. His jailer was a good man who had a daughter who was born blind. His jailer asked a favor of Valentinus. He said, "I see that you are a man of learning and know many things. My wife and I have a beautiful daughter who was born blind. Could you, would you teach her some of the things you know?"

Valentinus replied, "I will be glad to share with her what little knowledge I have. Bring her to me."

Soon Valentinus was teaching Julia, the jailer's daughter, about nature, mathematics, and God. Julia was a good and eager student. She trusted Valentinus and believed in everything he taught her. She saw the world through his eyes and his love for her. Through Valentinus' eyes, light entered Julia's eyes.

One day Julia asked him, "Valentinus, does God answer prayer?"

Valentinus answered, "God hears every prayer but may not answer every prayer the way people want their prayers answered."

"I pray every day that God will let me see the world you describe to me. Do you think I will ever be able to see?" she asked.

Valentinus answered, "God does what is best for us. We must believe in God and accept God's decision."

The two of them knelt and prayed in his prison cell. They were quiet a long time.

Suddenly Julia cried out, "I can see. Valentinus! I can see. God has heard my prayer and God has said 'Yes.'"

They both praised God and thanked God for the gift of sight.

Not too many days later Valentinus was executed for his belief in Jesus as God's Messiah and chosen one. The night before Valentinus' execution, he wrote Julia a letter urging her always to pray and to stay close to God and to follow the teachings of Jesus.

Valentinus was executed on February 14, 270 A.D. Julia planted a pink blossomed almond tree near his grave. Ever since, the almond tree has become a symbol of love and friendship in the Lord.

The Death of John the Baptist

The St. Barnabas Altarpiece, 1488, *Salome with the Baptist's head*

"Herod was afraid of John because he knew that John was a good and holy man, and so he kept him safe. He liked to listen to him, even though he became greatly disturbed every time he heard him."

Mark 6:20

Nugget

When we pray *Thy kingdom come,* we are praying that our little kingdoms and spheres of influence may perish so God's kingdom and rule can be established.

A Note Home:

Today your child learned of Jesus' sending out his 12 apostles, of the death of John the Baptist (Mark 6:6b-29), the legend of St. Valentine, the meaning of Thy kingdom come *in the Lord's Prayer. Love and service were discussed. You may wish to read pages 66-74 and continue studying Chapter 6 in* A Parent's Guide to Prayer.

Jesus – a Man of Sorrows

"He was despised and rejected by men; a man of sorrows, and acquainted with grief; and as one from whom men hide their faces he was despised, and we esteemed him not."

Isaiah 53:3

Albrecht Dürer, *Christ as a Man of Sorrows*

Nuggets

Jesus' *passion* refers to the suffering, both mental and physical that he endures before his death. In Caesarea Philippi, Jesus outlines the rest of his life. He says:

- The Son of Man must suffer much.
- The Son of Man will be rejected by the elders, chief priests, and teachers of the Law; i.e., all the important people.
- The Son of Man will be put to death.
- Three days later he will rise to new life.

As disciples of Jesus we must

- Deny ourselves
- Pick up our cross
- And follow Jesus.

Denial of self means we are to stop grasping for everything that will consume our lives and divert us from God's purposes for us in life.

The *cross* that disciples carry is in imitation of Jesus. Our lives should be devoted to carrying out Jesus' mission in this world.

Carrying Our Cross

"If anyone wants to come with me, … he must forget himself, carry his cross, and follow me. For whoever wants to save his own life will lose it; but whoever loses his life for me and for the gospel will save it."

Mark 8:34-35

JUST AS I AM, WITHOUT ONE PLEA

1. Just as I am, with-out one plea But that thy blood was shed for me, And that thou bidd'st me come to thee, O Lamb of God, I come, I come!
2. Just as I am, though tossed a-bout With man-y a con-flict, man-y a doubt, Fight-ings and fears with-in, with-out, O Lamb of God, I come, I come!
3. Just as I am, poor, wretch-ed, blind; Sight, rich-es, heal-ing of the mind; Yea, all I need in thee to find, O Lamb of God, I come, I come!
4. Just as I am, thou wilt re-ceive, Wilt wel-come, par-don, cleanse, re-lieve; Be-cause thy prom-ise I be-lieve, O Lamb of God, I come, I come!

Nugget

God's will is unity, peace, wholeness, joy, goodness, righteousness, purity, fidelity, love, hope, and faithfulness.

A Note Home:

Today your child learned about the church season of Lent, the cost of discipleship, Jesus' upcoming passion (Mark 8:27-38), and the meaning of Thy kingdom come, thy will be done on earth as it is in heaven *in the Lord's Prayer.*

How Much Land Does a Person Need?

Cast
Kathy, a farmer's wife
Eleanor, her sister
Paul, Kathy's husband
Mrs. Jones, a land owner
A farmer
A tradesman
Chief of Bashkirs
Narrator I
Narrator II

Act I

Narrator I: Our story opens with Eleanor, who lives in town. She is visiting her sister Kathy. The year is 1890. Kathy is married to a farmer and enjoys her life with him.

Eleanor: Really, my dear Kathy, how can you stand living here on the farm? You never get to go to any balls or hear any stimulating conversation. You don't even have nice clothes to wear. And you smell like the farm animals.

Kathy: What you say may be true, Eleanor. Our lives are much simpler than yours. But so are our wants. We have plenty of food, good shelter, and clothes on our back. We all work hard and sleep well at night. What more could we possibly want? At least our lives are honest lives.

Eleanor: Well, if you think feeding pigs and milking cows is a good life, you are welcome to it. You and your children will never enjoy elegance or manners. Too bad.

Kathy: I am not so sure city life is any better. You are surrounded by temptations. Your husband may take to drinking or chasing after women or gambling, and you will be ruined.

Narrator II: Paul, Kathy's husband, was resting in the next room. He overheard his wife's and Eleanor's conversation. He thought to himself, "It is true. Hard work keeps me from vice and putting nonsense into my head. But if I had more land, I would not be afraid of the Devil himself."

Narrator II: The Devil overheard Paul's thoughts and the women's conversation. He was pleased to hear Paul boast that if he had plenty of land he would not be afraid of him. The Devil decided to give Paul his wish so he could get Paul into his power.

How Much Land Does a Person Need?

Act II

Narrator I:	Not too many days later, Paul heard that Mrs. Jones, who owned a large farm, was selling her land.
Paul:	Mrs. Jones, I would like to buy some land from you. For how much are you selling your land? And would you let me pay 50 percent this year and 25 percent for each of the next two years?
Mrs. Jones:	I am selling my land for 100 rubles an acre. Yes, I will let you pay for half now and the rest over the next two years.
Paul:	Then I would like to buy 100 acres. Give me a few days to get the money together. May I have the southern portion of your land from the lake to the woods?
Mrs. Jones:	Yes, you may. I will wait.
Paul:	Kathy, Mrs. Jones has agreed to let me buy 100 acres for 100 rubles a piece.
Kathy:	Where are we going to get that type of money? We only have 1000 rubles not 10,000 rubles.
Paul:	I have a plan. We can put William out to work. He is almost 18 years old. His wages for the next three years can be advanced to us. That will make another 3,000 rubles. Then we can ask your sister's husband to loan us another 1,000 rubes. That will make 5,000 rubes. Mrs. Jones has agreed to take 50 percent now and the rest over the next two years.
Kathy:	Well, it sounds like a great opportunity. I will go in the morning to ask my sister to ask her husband for the money. You can take William and place him with the highest bidder.
Narrator II:	It wasn't long before Paul had 5,000 rubles. He and his family moved onto the land and built a small house for themselves and barn for his animals. Everyone worked hard, and they prospered. Sometimes the neighbors' cows got into the wheat field. Paul fenced in his property to keep them out but still they got in. Paul got more and more annoyed at his neighbors for allowing their cattle to invade his land. Then one day a farmer was passing through and asked if he could stay the night. During the evening meal, Paul and his family talked to the farmer.
Paul:	Where do you come from and where are you going?
Stranger:	Oh, I come from beyond the Volga. I moved there five years ago with a group of other settlers. We were each given 25 acres of ground. We did not have to buy it. The land was so fertile that our crops yielded three times the normal yield. Within five years I owned more than 500 acres. There is still much open land. But I cannot work any more land than 500 acres.
Narrator I:	Paul's heart leaped with desire. Later that night he said to Kathy:

How Much Land Does a Person Need?

Paul: Why should we live on 100 acres when we can have 500 acres? We can sell our farm for a profit, take what is free and buy 500 or 1,000 acres. Our children will work the farm, and we will hire some workmen as well. Within a few years, we will be rich.

Kathy: But Paul. This will be the second move within five years.

Paul: I know, I know. But this time we will really make it big. Why, within another five years, none of us will have to work.

Kathy: Paul, we are already rich. Why do we need anything more?

Paul: Trust me. Our past risk taking has paid off. This will be our last move.

Narrator II: Paul told Kathy his idea for getting rich. She finally agreed with him. After all, 100 acres is not much when you could have 500 or 1,000 acres. Paul left her to go buy this new land while Kathy began to sell everything and pack for the trip.

Narrator I: Paul and his family moved beyond the Volga River. They worked hard and prospered. Life was good to them. Then one day a tradesman passed through and asked to spend the night.

Paul: You are a stranger in these parts. Where do you come from?

Tradesman: Oh, I come from a land that belongs to the Bashkirs. They are tribesman and herders of sheep and goats. They do not work their land. And they are simple minded. For 1,000 rubles I bought 5,000 acres. They gave me a deed to the land, and now my family and I will be on easy street in a few years. I am on my way to buy farming tools and supplies.

Paul: Is there enough land for me, too?

Kathy: Oh, no you don't! We are not going to move again. Our children need some permanence. We have plenty right here. And I am not going to move.

Tradesman: You sound like my wife. She did not want to move. And even now she is not too happy. But I am sure within a year or so she will be.

Narrator II: That evening Kathy and Paul had a terrible argument. Kathy did not want to move again. Paul insisted that this move would be their last move, that he was going to buy land from the Bashkirs, and that she and the family will move with him. Paul left the next day with 1,000 rubles in his pockets and trinkets and gifts in his saddle bags.

How Much Land Does a Person Need?

Act III

Narrator I:	When Paul arrived in the land of the Bashkirs, he found everything as the tradesman had said. The Bashkirs were simple folk who did not work very hard. The men liked to sit around all day drinking tea and talking. Paul approached them.
Paul:	I hear that I can buy land from you. Your soil is rich. Please accept these gifts from me. What must I pay for your land?
Chief:	We thank you for your gifts. In return, you can have as much land as you wish for 1,000 rubles.
Paul:	As much land as I wish?
Chief:	Yes, as much land as you can walk in a day.
Paul:	There is no limit?
Chief:	You can only have as much land as you can mark off from sun up to sun down. If you do not return to your starting spot before the sun sets, you lose your money.
Paul:	I agree. I agree. But how will we know what land will be mine?
Chief:	You will take a shovel with you. Every time you turn, you are to dig a hole and pile up the turf. The next day we will go around and mark off your land. Now, I think you better get a good night's sleep.
Narrator I:	Paul and his servant, Sam, were led to their quarters. Paul was unable to sleep all night. He was calculating what distances he could walk in a day and how much land he would get for 1,000 rubles. Then he began to figure out what he would do with the land and how many cattle he would have.
Narrator II:	Just before morning, Paul fell asleep. He had a nightmare which awakened him. He dreamed that the Chief was laughing at him. When he got near to the Chief, he saw that the man was not the chiefbut the tradesman who told him about this land. He went over to touch the tradesman and found him to be the farmer who had told him about his land near the Volga. He, too, was laughing.He looked closer at the farmer. It was not the farmer but the Devil himself laughing as hard as he could looking at a man who laid face down on the ground. Paul turned the man over and saw him-self dead.

How Much Land Does a Person Need?

Act IV

Paul: I am not going to let that nightmare prevent me from securing my land. Why, this is an opportunity of a lifetime.

Narrator I: With that Paul got up, pulled his boots on, filled his water bag, and stuffed bread in his shirt. He awakened his servant, the Chief and his tribesman. They rode out to a spot on a piece of nar-row ground. As the sun was rising, Paul spoke to the Chief.

Paul: Here is my hat and 1,000 rubles. As soon as the sun comes up, I am off. I will be back before sunset.

Narrator II: Paul walked three miles quickly in one direction. He dug his turning mark hole and hurried for another five miles in another direction.

Paul: I think I had better take a short rest and eat something. That clump of trees over there looks great.I will make a wide circle around them before making my third turn. Well, I mustn't spend all day here. But it sure is getting hot. I will take off my shirt to cool down and will take another drink of water.

Narrator I: By early afternoon, the heat made Paul dizzy. He sat down and took off his boots. He rested for only a minute and then began racing again.

Paul: Oh, look at that sun, it is later than I think. I can barely see the Chief and the tribesman. It is so faraway. The sun waits for no man. I better hurry up. My feet are killing me. I should have left my boots on. I wish I hadn't been so greedy. My time is running out. I may lose my 1,000 rubles and my great opportunity if I do not hurry.

Narrator II: The walking became increasingly more difficult for Paul. His feet were bleeding. His chest ached. And he was dizzy.

Paul: I don't think I can go another step. Oh, God! Help me. I would be a fool to go all this distance and not to finish. It looks as though the sun is setting. But wait! I am down here and the hill is hiding the sun. The tribesmen are cheering me on. I can see my cap. I have plenty of land. But will God let me live on it? Have I lost my life? My chest is killing me.

Narrator I: Paul used what little strength he had left to climb the hill. He took a deep breath and climbed the hill. The tribesmen cheered him on. He reached the top and fell over on his cap and money before the sun set.

How Much Land Does a Person Need?

Paul: Why is that chief laughing so? Has all my labor been in vain?

Narrator II: Paul's servant ran over to him. He turned him over and saw that he was dead. The tribesmen clicked their tongues to show their pity.

Narrator I: Paul's servant picked up Paul's shovel and dug a grave twelve feet deep, six feet wide, and six feet long. That was all the land Paul needed.

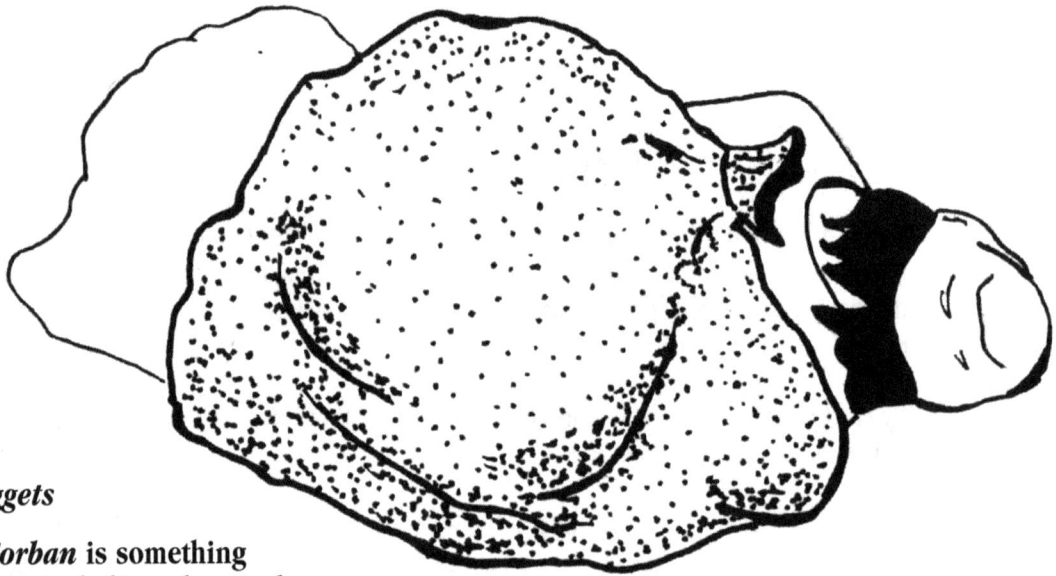

Nuggets

- *Corban* is something that is dedicated to God.

- *Pharisees* were a Jewish religious sect that believed in the immortality of the soul, in the resurrection of the body, and in the existence of spirits. They believed that people are rewarded or punished in their future life according to how they lived on earth.

- *Herodians* were a political group that supported Herod and hoped for a restoration of the Jewish state.

A Note Home

Today your child participated in the play How Much Land Does a Person Need?, *learned of the growing opposition to* Jesus' ministry, the feeding of the 4,000 (Mark 8:1-26) and the meaning of Give us this day our daily bread *in the Lord's Prayer.*

The Prodigal Son Returns Home

"I have sinned against God and against you.
I am no longer fit to be called your son."

Luke 15:18

Rembrandt, *The Prodigal Son*

"If you forgive others the wrongs they have done to
you, your Father in heaven will also forgive you. But
if you do not forgive others, then your Father will
not forgive the wrongs you have done."

Matthew 6:14

A Note Home:

   Today your child learned The Parable of the Prodigal Son (Luke 15:11-32), about forgiveness, and the meaning of
And forgive us our trespasses, As we forgive those who trespass against *us in the Lord's Prayer.*

Forgiveness is Important for Spiritual Wholeness

1. Somebody has done something terrible to you. You have two possible reactions. You can either forgive or not forgive the person who has wronged you.

2. Martin Luther King, Jr. said:

   Mindful that hate is an evil and a dangerous force, we too often think of what it does to the person hated. But there is another side we must never overlook. Hate is just as injurious to the person who hates. Like an unchecked cancer, hate corrodes the personality and eats away its vital unity.

   What does Martin Luther King, Jr. mean? Why would he know so much about hate?

3. What can happen to people who do not forgive others?

   They will develop an extreme dislike or hate towards the person who did them wrong.

   Their dislike or hate will grow in them like unchecked yeast. This growth can shut out other growth factors such as love.

   Lack of love coupled with dislike and hate can create mental depression, which makes people feel unhappy all the time.

   Negative thinking people see the dark side of things.

   If people make up their minds not to forgive one person, it is easier the next time someone does them wrong not to forgive that person. Soon they will have a long list of people they dislike or hate. And they, not the hated object, are being destroyed. Why?

4. There are always obstacles to forgiveness.

   It is difficult to forget what has been done to you. Perhaps you should not forget the experience. Instead learn from it and grow. It is important to know which people you can trust and which people you cannot trust. But you still must forgive the offender.

   Pride often prevents people from asking for forgiveness. How did Edmund's pride get him deeper into trouble?

   Forgiveness may take time, prayer, and God's help for you to achieve.

5. Forgiveness helps us to live better lives.

   Forgiveness frees us from dislike, hate, and revenge and allows us to live a life of hope, love, and happiness.

   Forgiveness allows us to have a good relationship with God.

   A prayer from Isaiah 55:7-11

   Turn to the Lord and pray to him, now that he is near.

   Let the wicked leave their way of life and change their way of thinking.

   Let them turn to the Lord, our God; he is merciful and quick to forgive.

   "My thoughts," says the Lord, "are not like yours, and my ways are different from yours.

   As high as the heavens are above the earth,

   so high are my ways and thoughts above yours.

   "My word is like the snow and the rain that come down from the sky to water the earth.

   They make the crops grow and provide seed for planting and food to eat.

   So also will be the word that I speak—it will not fail to do what I plan for it; it will do everything I send it to do."

The Temple of the Lord

- Herod rebuilt the Temple. Work began on it in 20 B.C. and was completed in 26 A.D., a period of 46 years.

- The Temple stands in the center of the rectangle. Only priests were allowed to step inside this inner building.

- The large area surrounding the Temple is called the Court of Gentiles.

- Under the colonnades surrounding the Court of the Gentiles, rabbis use to teach their followers.

- There were at least seven entrances to the Court of Gentiles. A few are illustrated here.

- The pinnacle of the Temple is to the lower left of the building.

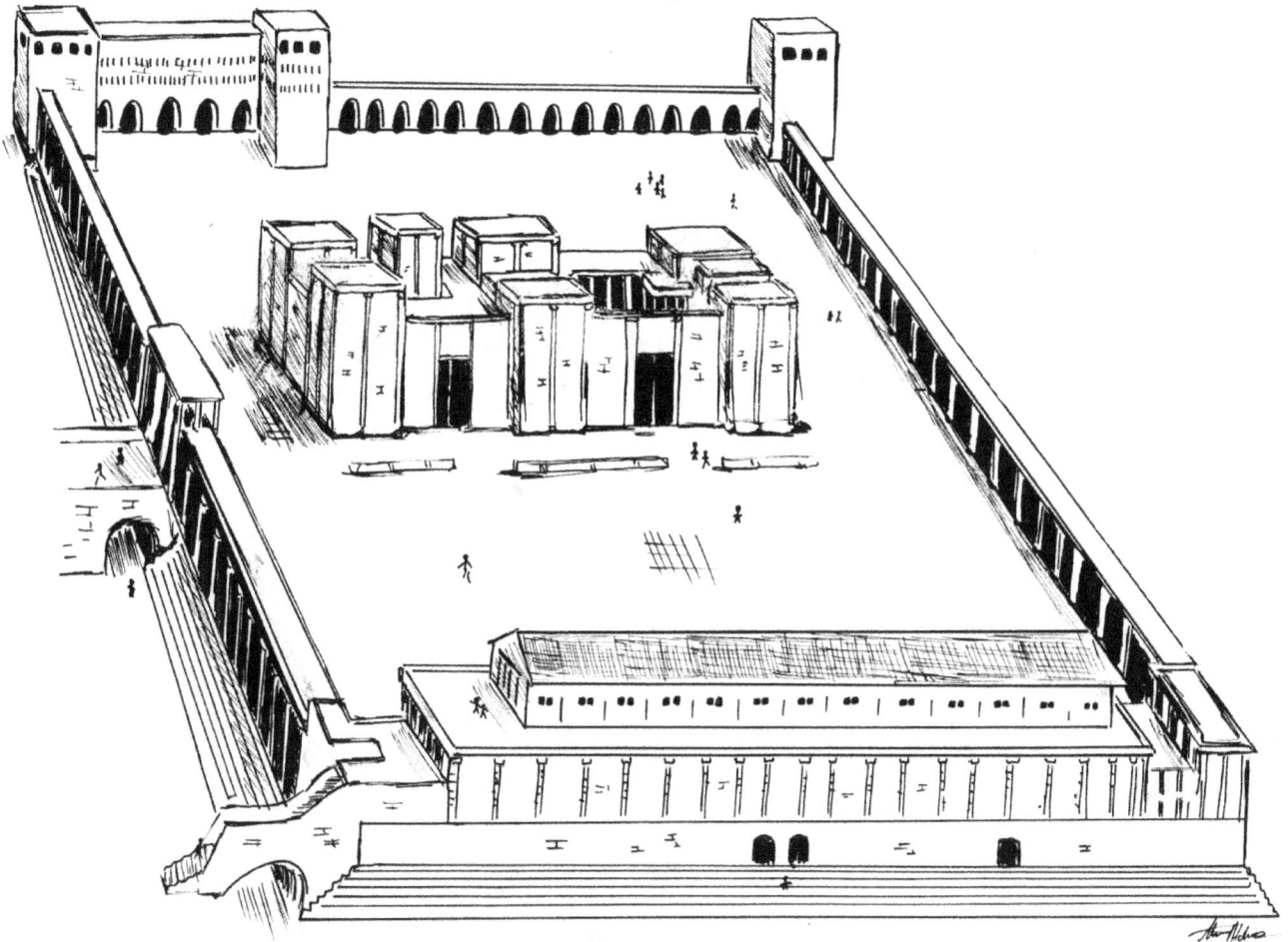

The Temple and our churches are holy places. They are places that have been set aside for the worship of God. Jesus objected to the misuse of this holy space. He said, "My Temple will be called a house of prayer for the people of all nations. But you have turned it into a hideout for thieves!"

Mark 11:17

Money Has Many Faces

A Note Home:

    Today your child learned of Jesus' entrance into Jerusalem, his love for Jerusalem, his cleansing of the Temple, and his righteous anger (Mark 11:1-26 and Luke 13:31-35). Your child's class made up a game about being moneychangers in the Temple.

The Parable of the Wicked Tenants

"This is the owner's son. Come on, let's kill him, and his property will be ours!".... "What then, will the owner of the vineyard do?" asked Jesus. "He will come and kill those men and turn the vineyard over to other tenants."

Mark 12:7 and 9

"Pay to the Emperor what belongs to the Emperor, and pay to God what belongs to God."

Mark 12:47

PSALM 24—FLING WIDE THE GATES

The world and all that is in it belong to the Lord;

the earth and all who live on it are his.

He built it on the deep waters beneath the earth

and laid its foundations in the ocean depths.

Who has the right to go up the Lord's hill? Who may enter his holy Temple?

Those who are pure in act and in thought, who do not worship idols or make false promises.

The Lord will bless them and save them; God will declare them innocent.

Such are the people who come to God, who come into the presence of the God of Jacob.

Fling wide the gates, open the ancient doors, and the great king will come in.

Who is this great king?

He is the Lord, strong and mighty, the Lord, victorious in battle.

Fling wide the gates, open the ancient doors, and the great king will come in.

Who is this great king?

The triumphant Lord—he is the great king!

A Note Home:

Today your child learned The Parable of the Wicked Tenants in the Vineyard, how it compared to Jesus' time and our time, the consequences involved then and now, and rendering to Caesar what belongs to Caesar and to God what belongs to God (Mark 12:1-17). Then we discussed Psalm 24.

The Passion Begins

"We all must be servants to each other. No one is greater and better than someone else."

Adaptation of John 13:16.

"The sorrow in my heart is so great that it almost crushes me. Stay here and keep watch."

Mark 14:34

Stanley Spencer, 1920, *Last Supper*

LET US BREAK BREAD TOGETHER

Negro Spiritual

Unison

1. Let us break bread to-geth-er on our knees;
2. Let us drink wine to-geth-er on our knees;
3. Let us praise God to-geth-er on our knees;

Let us break bread to-geth-er on our knees.
Let us drink wine to-geth-er on our knees.
Let us praise God to-geth-er on our knees.

When I fall on my knees, with my face to the ris-ing sun,

O Lord, have mer-cy on me.

Prayer of Thanksgiving

We give thanks, Almighty God, that you have been present to us in Jesus Christ. Strengthen our faith, increase our love for one another, and send us forth into the world in courage and peace, rejoicing in the power of the Holy Spirit, through Jesus Christ our Lord. Amen.

Prayer of Confession

Almighty and most merciful God, we have erred and strayed from your ways like lost sheep.

We have followed too much the devices and desires of our own hearts.

We have offended against your holy laws.

We have left undone those things which we ought to have done, and we have done those things which we ought not to have done.

Have mercy upon us.

Spare those, O God, who confess their faults.

Restore those who are penitent, according to the promises declared to all persons in Christ Jesus.

And grant, O most merciful God, for Jesus' sake, that we may hereafter live a godly, righteous, and sober life, to the glory of your holy name.

Amen.

Giovanni Bellini, 1460, *The Agony in the Garden*

Nuggets

- **Kneeling is a position of servitude.**

- **The Last Supper is Jesus' last meal with his disciples on Maundy Thursday.**

- **Holy Communion, Holy Eucharist, or the Lord's Supper is a sacrament of the church and a remembrance of Jesus' Last Supper. Believers meet Jesus through the bread and wine and are united with him in their ordinary life.**

A Note Home:

   Today your child learned about Jesus' Last Supper, Judas' betrayal, and Jesus' agony in the Garden of Gethsemane. We tried to relive some of the events of that night by having a foot washing and a reenactment of the Last Supper. Scripture references were Mark 14:1-11; 14:32-42.

The Betrayal of Jesus

The Betrayal of Jesus, a 12th-century anonymous painting, shows Peter cutting off Malchus' ear.

Christ Before Caiaphas

Gerrit van Honthorst, *Christ Before Caiaphas*

Nuggets

- The *Sanhedrin* was the court in Jerusalem that governed Jewish religious and political life during and before the New Testament era. It was under Roman domination and consisted of 71 members presided over by a High Priest who cooperated with Roman authorities.

- *Blasphemy* is speaking disrespectfully about God. The Jewish people did not believe that Jesus was God's son or from God. When Jesus said that he was the Son of God, they considered Jesus to be disrespectful and a liar. Jesus was believed to be a blasphemer. Blasphemers were subject to the death penalty.

Peter's Denial

Anonymous, after the manner of Caravaggesque, *Peter's Denial*

THE LORD'S PRAYER

- The first section of the Lord's Prayer concerns God's will and God's point of view.

- The second half of the Lord's Prayer, beginning with *Give us this day our daily bread,* concerns our needs.

  - Notice how the Lord's Prayer provides a framework for right living.

  - We can begin overcoming the evil in the world by worshiping God.

  - We can try to do God's will by only asking for and being satisfied with our daily bread.

  - We are to seek forgiveness from God and others.

  - We are to recognize our need for God's help in avoiding temptation which could lead us into evil.

  - We are to sing God's praises and recognize God's rule over us.

- Amen=And so shall it be.

WERE YOU THERE?

Negro Spiritual

1. Were you there when they cru-ci-fied my Lord?(Were you there?)Were you
2. Were you there when they nailed Him to the tree?(Were you there?)Were you
3. Were you there when they pierced Him in the side?(Were you there?)Were you
4. Were you there when they laid Him in the tomb?(Were you there?)Were you

there when they cru-ci-fied my Lord? (my Lord) Oh! . . . . .
there when they nailed Him to the tree? (the tree) Oh! . . . . .
there when they pierced Him in the side? (the side) Oh! . . . . .
there when they laid Him in the tomb? (the tomb) Oh! . . . . .

. . . . Some-times it caus-es me to trem-ble, trem-ble,
. . . . Some-times it caus-es me to trem-ble, trem-ble,
. . . . Some-times it caus-es me to trem-ble, trem-ble,
. . . . Some-times it caus-es me to trem-ble, trem-ble,

trem-ble; Were you there when they cru-ci-fied my Lord?
trem-ble; Were you there when they nailed Him to the tree?
trem-ble; Were you there when they pierced Him in the side?
trem-ble; Were you there when they laid Him in the tomb?

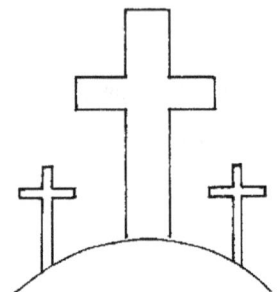

A Note Home:

Today your child learned of Judas' kiss of betrayal, Jesus' appearance before the Sanhedrin (Mark 14:43-72); dis-cussed feelings and thoughts on abandonment, denial, and evil. S/he also learned the meaning of the petition And lead us not into temptation, But deliver us from evil *in the Lord's Prayer.*

Good Friday Events

Spanish statue of the Scourged Jesus.

Scourges were whips of cords or knotted cord often weighted with pieces of metal or bone. The victim was often stripped and his hands were tied to a post with leather thongs during the beating. It was customary to scourge a condemned prisoner before crucifying him.

Albrecht Dürer, *Jesus' Carries His Cross*

Good Friday Events

Andrea Mantegna, 1456-59, *Crucifixion*

Crucifixion was reserved by the Romans for low class criminals, foreigners, and slaves. The Roman cross consisted of two beams. Jesus carried the cross beam. Those being crucified were either lashed or nailed to the cross. On the upright portion of the cross, there was a projecting peg to bear some of the person's weight so as to prevent the nailed victim's body from tearing away from the cross. Death by crucifixion was protracted. Dehydration, loss of blood, hunger, and exhaustion are the direct cause of death and not crucifixion. The only relief permitted a victim was a stupefying draught. It sometimes took three or four days for death to occur.

But he endured the suffering that should have been ours, the pain that we should have borne. All the while we thought that his suffering was punishment sent by God. But because of our sins he was wounded, beaten because of the evil we did. We are healed by the punishment he suffered, made whole by the blows he received. All of us were like sheep that were lost, each of us going his own way. But the Lord made the punishment fall on him, the punishment all of us deserved.

Isaiah 53:4-6

In the same way the chief priests and the teachers of the Law made fun of Jesus, saying to one another, "He saved others, but he cannot save himself! Let us see the Messiah, the king of Israel, come down from the cross now, and we will believe in him!"

Mark 15:31-32

A Note Home:

   Today your child learned of Jesus' appearance before Pilate, Pilate's attempts to release him, Pilate's reasons for sentencing Jesus, Jesus' scourging and trip to the cross, his death on the cross (Mark 15:1-41; Luke 23:32-34). The class also broke into groups to rank people's guilt on having Jesus crucified.

Good Friday Events

Pietro Lorenzetti,
1320-30, *Descent
from the Cross*

"He went into the presence of Pilate and asked for the body of Jesus. Then he took the body down, wrapped it in a linen sheet, and placed it in a tomb which had been dug out of solid rock and which had never been used."

Luke 23:52-3

And even the angels weep.

Carlo Crivelli, *Pieta.*

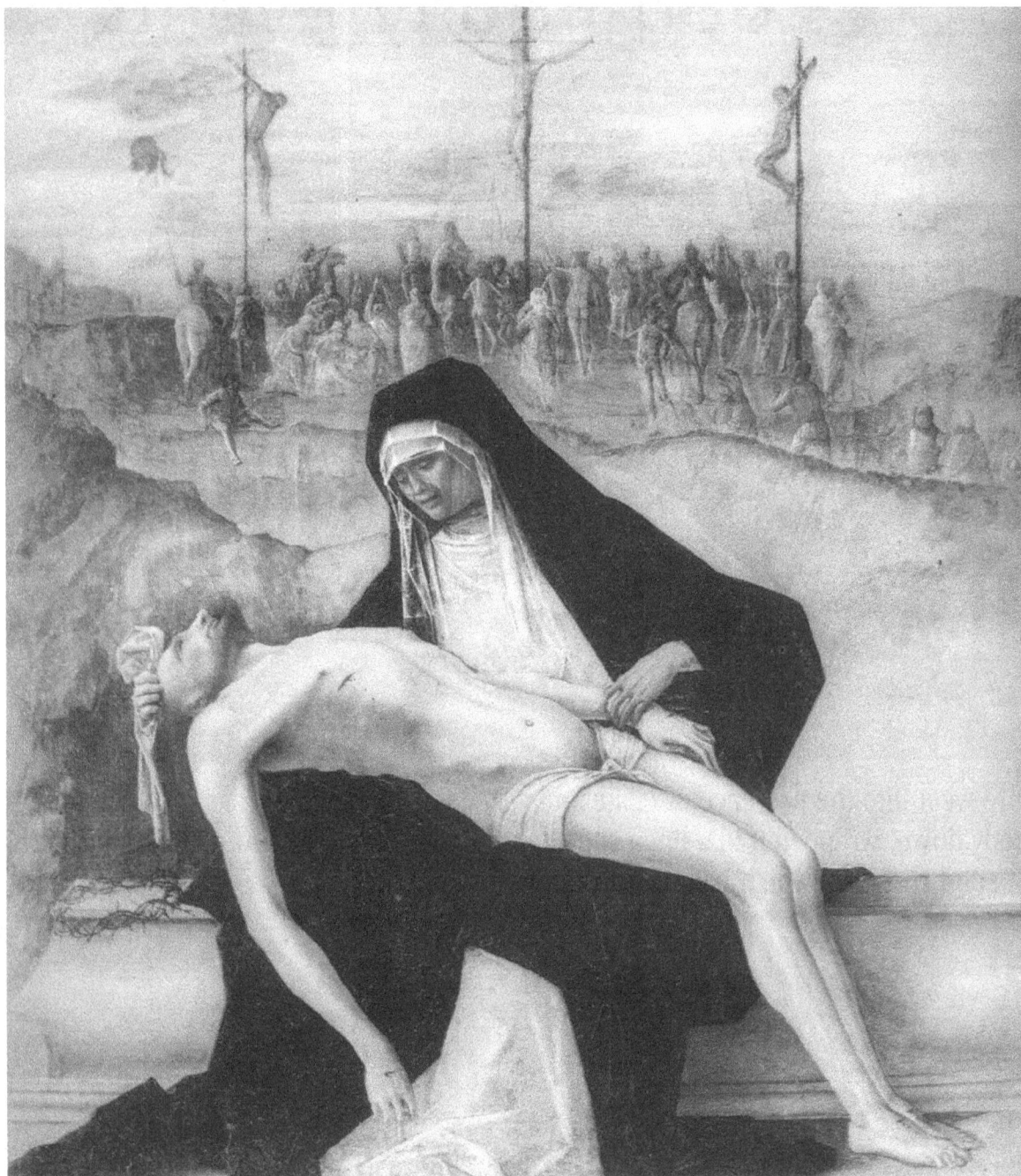

Ercole Roberti, *Pieta*

"At the time of Jesus' circumcision, the old man Simeon said to Mary, 'This child is chosen by God for the destruction and the salvation of many in Israel. He will be a sign from God which many people will speak against and so reveal their secret thoughts. And sorrow like a sharp sword, will break your own heart.'"

Luke 2:34-5

Jesus' Burial

Berlin-Dahlem, *Preparations for the Entombment of Christ*

Note Mary who has fainted in the pathway to the right, John who
stands facing the women, and Job who leans against the tree.

CHRIST THE LORD IS RISEN TODAY

1. "Christ the Lord is risen to - day," Al - le - lu - ia!
2. Vain the stone, the watch, the seal; Al - le - lu - ia!
3. Lives a - gain our glo - rious King; Al - le - lu - ia!
4. Soar we now where Christ has led, Al - le - lu - ia!
5. Hail, the Lord of earth and heaven! Al - le - lu - ia!

Sons of men and an - gels say; Al - le - lu - ia!
Christ has burst the gates of hell: Al - le - lu - ia!
Where, O death, is now thy sting? Al - le - lu - ia!
Fol - lowing our ex - alt - ed Head; Al - le - lu - ia!
Praise to Thee by both be given; Al - le - lu - ia!

Raise your joys and tri - umphs high; Al - le - lu - ia!
Death in vain for - bids His rise; Al - le - lu - ia!
Once He died, our souls to save; Al - le - lu - ia!
Made like Him, like Him we rise; Al - le - lu - ia!
Thee we greet tri - um - phant now; Al - le - lu - ia!

Sing, ye heavens, and earth, re - ply; Al - le - lu - ia!
Christ has o - pened par - a - dise. Al - le - lu - ia!
Where thy vic - to - ry, O grave? Al - le - lu - ia!
Ours the cross, the grave, the skies. Al - le - lu - ia!
Hail, the Res - ur - rec - tion Thou! Al - le - lu - ia! A-MEN.

"There was a garden in the place where Jesus had been put to death, and in it there was a new tomb where no one had ever been buried. Since it was the day before the Sabbath and because the tomb was close by, they placed Jesus' body there."

John 19:41-42

A Note Home:

Today your child learned about Jesus' descent from the cross, his burial, people's grief and anxiety, and about Jesus' resurrection. Scripture references were Matthew 27:57-61; Mark 15:42-47; Luke 23:50-56; 24:1-12; John 19:38-20:18.

Christ Appearing to His Mother

Rogier van der Weyden, 1440-5, *Christ Appearing to His Mother*

Did Jesus Really Rise from the Dead?

Many people like to say that Jesus was somehow resuscitated and therefore freed himself from his prison tomb. What do you think? Be sure to take into consideration:

• Jesus' physical condition—he had been scourged, beaten, crowned with thorns, nailed to a cross, speared through his side, and had not eaten or drunk anything in over three days.

• Even if Jesus were resuscitated, would he have had the strength to unwrap his grave clothes, roll the stone away from the tomb's entrance, and overpower his guards?

Jesus' disciples have been accused of taking his body. Consider:

• These men were frightened men in hiding. They deserted Jesus. Jesus was dead. Why would they risk their lives to get Jesus' dead body?

• These men did not even make any attempt to bury Jesus because they were so frightened.

Other people like to say that the Romans took Jesus' body. Why would they do such a thing?

• The Romans were not interested in Jesus.

• What interest would they have in a decomposing body?

• If any of Jesus' enemies wanted to stamp out Jesus' followers and what they were proclaiming, all they would have had to do is to produce his body.

When you consider all the possibilities for what happened to Jesus' body, it is difficult not to believe the biblical record about Jesus' resurrection. Jesus lives! What does his resurrection mean to you?

A Note Home:

Today your child learned more about Jesus' resurrection and the arguments commonly used against such a possibility (Mark 16:1-8). The rest of the time was spent playing Bible Bowl.

Miracles and Life's Interruptions

Rembrandt, *Jesus Heals the Bleeding Woman*

"My daughter, your faith has made you well. Go in peace, and be healed of your trouble."

Mark 5:34

Nugget

The Jewish people during Jesus' time believed that a person was not whole unless their body and soul were well. They sought wholeness and peace or shalom. That is why Jesus first emphasized that the sick woman go in peace. Her spiritual life is more important than her physical condition.

DAY BY DAY

"My whole life I have been complaining that my work was constantly interrupted until I discovered that my interruptions were my work."

Henri Nouwen, *Reaching Out*

Day by day, Day by day,

Oh, dear Lord, three things I pray:

To see thee more clearly,

Love thee more dearly,

Follow thee more nearly,

Day by day.

Repeat

Kariye Camii, Istanbul, 14th century mural, *Jesus Raises Jairus' Daughter*

A Note Home:

Today we learned about two of Jesus' miracles (Mark 5:21-43) and how the interruptions in life very often may be our life's work. We began reading The Other Wise Man *and how his interruption to save a sick and needy man caused him to miss joining the other three wise men in their visit with the baby Jesus.*

Last Judgment

Michelangelo, 1536-41, *Last Judgment*

Benjamin West

"I was hungry and you fed me, thirsty and you gave me a drink; I was a stranger and you received me in your homes, naked and you clothed me; I was sick and you took care of me, in prison and you visited me."

Matthew 25:35-36

A Note Home:

Today your child heard the conclusion of The Other Wise Man, *of his discipleship, love and devotion to other people and compared his story with Matthew's Final Judgment (25:31-46).*

A Prison

Ginvanni Battista Paranesi, c. 1745, *A Prison*

"The Word was the source of life, and this life brought light to mankind. The light shines in the darkness, and the darkness has never put it out."

John 1:4-5

Nuggets

- A Christian allegory tells a "story in which people, things, and happenings have a hidden or symbolic Christian meaning. Christian allegories are used for teaching or explaining Christian ideas and moral principles" (*New World Dictionary*).

- Miracles are difficult for people to understand because

  - Miracles contradict natural law or the known laws of nature.

  - Christians believe that the miracles Jesus performed were caused by God through Jesus.

  - Most of Jesus' miracles required belief or faith on the part of the one to be healed.

  - Miracles send us a message from God. It is for us to determine what that message is.

A Note Home:

   Today your child heard the first part of a Christian allegory by John Aurelio called Simple Simon or Are the Stars Out Tonight? *This story was compared with Jesus' ministry and the opposition arrayed against him (John 1:1-13).*

The Time is Ripe

Constantin von Mitschke-Collande, 1919, *The Time is Ripe*

"As he was blessing them, he departed from them and was taken up into heaven. They worshiped him and went back into Jerusalem, filled with great joy, and spent all their time in the Temple giving thanks to God."

Luke 24:51-52.

Jesus
miracles
Creator
Redeemer
Sustainer
crucified
belief

risen
buried
cross
deny
follow
slavery

JESUS IS THE LIGHT OF THE WORLD

```
D O E E G V H C A R A H P S
R U Y N E D J M R G L Q P U
E P C I M P C A A O I U K S
M I R A C L E S E T S I Y T
M H U A P E A J O R H S B A
C N E S I R V N E K L E B I
O L I A O B C M U S Z F U N
A S F S R V E A G E U M R E
W D E B X E I L R R N S I R
O P S F D D N A I K O X E N
L J H E V B T U Q E I F D G
L C R E A T O R G J F Q S A
O X G A G S L A V E R Y W L
F H V Y C R U C I F I E D Y
```

A Note Home:

   Today we concluded our Christian allegory Simple Simon or Are the Stars Out Tonight? *and compared it to Jesus' ministry and the unbelief of the Pharisees and the teachers of the Law. Scriptural texts were John 1:1-13.*

www.ingramcontent.com/pod-product-compliance
Lightning Source LLC
Chambersburg PA
CBHW080936040426
42443CB00015B/3438